This book belongs to

Neris and India's Idiot-Proof Diet Cookbook

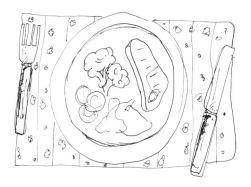

Bee Rawlinson, India Knight & Neris Thomas

FIG TREE

AN IMPRINT OF PENGUIN BOOKS

FIG TREE

Published by the Penguin Group

Penguin Books Ltd, 80 Strand, London WC2R ORL, England

Penguin Group (USA) Inc., 375 Hudson Street, New York, New York 10014, USA

Penguin Group (Canada), 90 Eglinton Avenue East, Suite 700, Toronto, Ontario,
    Canada M4P 2Y3 (a division of Pearson Penguin Canada Inc.)

Penguin Ireland, 25 St Stephen's Green, Dublin 2, Ireland (a division of Penguin
    Books Ltd)

Penguin Group (Australia), 250 Camberwell Road, Camberwell, Victoria 3124,
    Australia (a division of Pearson Australia Group Pty Ltd)

Penguin Books India Pvt Ltd, 11 Community Centre, Panchsheel Park,
    New Delhi – 110 017, India

Penguin Group (NZ), 67 Apollo Drive, Rosedale, North Shore 0632, New Zealand
    (a division of Pearson New Zealand Ltd)

Penguin Books (South Africa) (Pty) Ltd, 24 Sturdee Avenue, Rosebank,
    Johannesburg 2196, South Africa

Penguin Books Ltd, Registered Offices: 80 Strand, London WC2R ORL, England

www.penguin.com

First published 2008

4

Copyright © Bee Rawlinson, Neris Thomas and India Knight, 2008
Illustrations copyright © Neris Thomas, 2008

The moral right of the authors has been asserted

Set in Plantin and Thesis Sans
Designed by Smith & Gilmour, London
Printed in Italy by Printer Trento

A CIP catalogue record for this book is available from the British Library

ISBN: 978-1-905-49035-6

**This diet is not suitable for pregnant or nursing women, children, diabetics
or people with kidney disease. It is not entirely impossible to follow if you are
vegetarian, but it is not by any means vegetarian-friendly. Always consult your
doctor before embarking on a new eating plan. If you are diabetic, we very
highly recommend Dr Richard K. Bernstein's *The Diabetes Diet***

CONTENTS

CHAPTER ONE

INTRODUCTION

Neris' Fav

Hello, and thank you for buying this book. It came about in a very pleasing way, which we shall now share with you. When *Neris and India's Idiot-Proof Diet* was first published, we thought we'd start a blog to go with it. We imagined we'd get about fifty regulars, and that it would be cosy and nice, and that we'd chat among ourselves about green leafy veg and the best, least stodgy sausages. Instead, as the book crept up the bestseller chart, we very quickly started getting tens of thousands of hits a day – so many that we ditched the blog, which had become unmanageable, and turned it into a forum (which is still going strong, and which you can find at www.pig2twig.co.uk).

And one day, on this forum, there appeared a woman called Bee (cue halo of light and choirs of angels), who said she was a keen cook and had been playing about with recipes. Did we mind if she posted some of them? Of course not, we said – post away. Now, we all know that low-carb diets work, and we also all know that low-carb cooking is a bit of a faff: you have to be unusually creative to make it exciting, more creative than most of us are capable of being when it comes to cookery. So, to be perfectly frank, we expected Bee's recipes to be variants of meat in a cream sauce with a side of more meat. That's what most low-carb cookbooks are about, after all; they're effective, but they hardly get you drooling with anticipation. Quite the opposite, actually; we've read a fair few, and we sometimes put them down feeling slightly nauseous (especially if they involve ingenious new uses for pork scratchings. Sorry, but … gag).

Bee quietly started posting recipes. They weren't just good, or just appetizing: they completely blew our socks off. They weren't sad little approximations of 'normal' recipes. They were, well, amazing. They were so good that their low-carb aspect became irrelevant: they are simply recipes for absolutely delicious food that anyone would be delighted to eat, regardless of whether they are following our low-carb eating plan – a fact which was brought home to me (India) when I made my first ever batch of Bee's Onion bhajias, only to have my teenage sons demolish the whole lot and beg me to make them again the next day. Also, well – onion bhajias. It's hardly deprivation, is it?

The recipes kept coming, and they kept being brilliant. The thousands of women on our forum found them brilliant too. We printed them all out and kept them by the cooker; sometimes they were all we cooked for days on end. It made sense to share the goodness, and so here we are today: what you are holding is a handful of our own recipes, and all of Bee's. Ours are nice. Hers are stunning – and I (India) write as someone who is really devoted to cookery books, to the point of reading them in bed, so when I say these recipes can hold their own in the most exalted company, I mean it. Bee is the Nigella of low-carb. She's a genius. And her recipes work beautifully, rather like Delia's: they just don't go wrong, and they taste unbelievably good.

Now, some random points.

1 We wanted this book to be as user-friendly as possible. We know, for instance, that lots of people find breakfast a bit of a challenge when they're low-carbing – the combination of being in a hurry in the mornings and not necessarily having the stomach for yet more eggs and bacon can be problematic, especially when we consider breakfast to be the most important meal of the day. It's not a problem any more: we defy anyone not to find the recipes in these pages majorly appetizing.

2 All cookbooks cater to families, and this one does too. But it deviates from the norm in that it also caters to single people, or just knackered ones, who don't have the time or energy to make themselves a supper that involves forty-five minutes' work and three different pans. If you live alone and this rings a bell, you're going to be very happy: there are tons of recipes in here that you can throw together in minutes and that involve very little washing up.

3 Conversely, if there are lots of you and you don't fancy cooking yourself a different supper from your family's – rejoice. Like we were saying above, this is just good food. There's no reason why you shouldn't serve it up as a family meal. If you have ravenous teenagers in the house, just make them a side of mash or rice or whatever. But it may not be necessary: our recipes are not only yummy, but generously portioned and pretty filling.

Now, a word of warning. We've written an entire diet book, and we strongly advise you to buy it. Yes, we would say that. But it's true, and it's important. You could cobble together a version of our diet from the information contained in the pages of the book you're holding, but it wouldn't give you the full picture, there would be tons of information you'd be missing out on, and you wouldn't lose weight as spectacularly and efficiently as you would – as you will – if you read the diet book first. At the time of writing, the women (and handful of men) on our forum have lost a collective 4 tonnes – 4 tonnes! – by following our eating plan. It absolutely and categorically works, but if you want it to work for you, you need to read the manual. This cookbook is a companion volume. It isn't the diet. If you want to do the diet, buy the diet book.

Another word of warning – and this is very important. If you eat the recipes in this book with a side of carb, you will actively get fat, even if the carb is a supposedly 'healthy' one. Also, if you are new to the diet and you start cooking everything in this book and shoving it down you, you won't lose weight properly. It makes sense: eat onion bhajias three times a day, and you're unlikely to see dramatic movement on the scales. Once a day is great. But the first and strictest phase of our diet involves basing your intake of food around lean protein, good fat and green vegetables for the first fortnight, and this is the most effective way of kick-starting dramatic weight loss. Refer to the book for blow-by-blow instructions on how to do this: if your idea of dieting involves restricting calories, you're going to get confused unless you have all the information in front of you. Plus, we have lots to say about supplements, sweeteners, alcohol and so on, and you need to take it all on board before you start.

Which leads me neatly on to quantities. Here's what I posted up on our forum. This is the most indulgent, luxurious way of eating imaginable – but it isn't magic. You need to use common sense, too. Using a generous splash of double cream to make a sauce or gravy is fine; whipping up half a litre to eat with a spoon isn't. Apologies if this strikes you as painfully obvious, but the forum has taught us that what is obvious to one person isn't necessarily remotely obvious to another. So: quantities.

A word about quantities, since it's a subject that keeps coming up. Please use your common sense. If you eat a block of cheese a day, you're not going to lose weight. A couple of spoonfuls of mayonnaise turned into a dressing is fine, sitting down and polishing off half a jar isn't. Other than meat and fish, everything – including green vegetables – has a carb content. We don't believe in counting anything, but we do expect you to have a think about portion sizes. No diet is so magical that you can eat unlimited amounts of food and still lose weight. You can eat delicious things on this diet, but there are still limits.

Eat off a normal dinner plate, not off a tray (or from a trough). Base your meal around protein and green leafy veg. Have a big steak (or whatever) if you're hungry, but don't go overboard and have six Giant Haystacks-sized helpings of whatever you're having on the side, and then be all surprised when you're not losing weight.

Have a handful of nuts a day and a couple of pieces of cheese – each piece should be roughly half the size of the palm of your hand (though NB your mileage may vary – some people can eat more than this, no problem, some can't – trial and error).

Cream is absolutely fine used as a condiment, in sauces or whatever, but obviously whipping up a family-sized tub with some Splenda is not going to speed things up – au contraire.

Ditto butter: use it for cooking, but don't snack on slabs of it.
And so on. It's all pretty obvious, really, but having been away
for a week and had a read around the forum this morning I
(India) think it probably needs reiterating.

Eat until you're full, not until you're absolutely stuffed. Think
about what you're putting in your mouth. Don't confuse thirst
with hunger. And don't eat like a fat person – cramming
everything you can lay your hands on down your gullet, even
if it's all low-carb. YOU ARE NOT THE BIN, so don't treat
yourself as though you are. The whole point of the exercise is
to dump the fat person habits, as well as the fat person shape.

Finally, I can't say this enough – wine slows you down, and can
stall you. If you're going to drink, train yourself to drink clear
spirits. If you must have wine, understand that you're trading
faster weight loss for a night in with a bottle of white. Half of
that bottle of white is sugar, so OBVIOUSLY it's going to have
an impact.

As for the odd stray: it may not show up on the scales today,
but it will tomorrow or next week. Cheat if you must, but accept
there will be consequences.

We lost 10 stone between us by following this way of eating – and, more to the point, we've kept it off nearly two years later. In my case (India), Bee's recipes have helped more than I can say – it's hard to feel deprived when you're eating food that is this delicious. We'd like to say a giant thank you to her, and to all the wonderful people on our forum, who've made us laugh and cry over the past year, who've shared their stories with dazzling honesty, and who have given us the most fascinating insight into how, and why, people overeat. As we wrote in *Neris and India's Idiot-Proof Diet*, being fat sucks. The brilliant thing is, you can get un-fat, like we did and like tens of thousands of our followers (ooh! A cult!) have. Best of luck to you all, and bon appétit!

India Knight and Neris Thomas
July 2007

CHAPTER TWO
THE GOLDEN RULES

1 You must drink at least 8 large glasses of water a day.
This is a bare minimum. Try to aim for 12, and 15 wouldn't hurt.
It sounds odd, and like clichéd women's-magazine stuff, but if
you don't do this you will lose weight at a far slower rate than if
you do. You are also more likely to be constipated, and your skin
may mess up. So go for it: the more you drink, the faster you lose
and the better you feel. Have a 1.5 litre bottle of mineral water
next to you at work, and drink from it throughout the day. When
it's gone, feel free to start (if not finish) another one, so you're
drinking up to 3 litres.

2 You absolutely must have breakfast, lunch and dinner.
On this diet, unlike on the usual calorie-controlled diets, not
eating actively counts against you, and slows weight loss down.
Skipping breakfast is forbidden. Seriously: if you skip a meal,
your weight loss will be dramatically slower than if you eat
three times a day.

**3 It is crucial to eat a combination of good fats and
protein at every meal** – so dress your salad, sauce your
steak, have your prawns dunked in (preferably home-made)
mayonnaise. The combination of fat and protein creates weight
loss with this way of eating.

**4 Don't make the mistake of thinking that 'dieting' means
'low-fat'.** If you try to do your own, low-fat version of this diet,
you won't lose the weight. If you're having three meals a day and
you still feel hungry, then for heaven's sake EAT. Have a snack.
Or two, or three. Don't graze all day, obviously. But don't go
hungry either.

**5 You must have a couple of handfuls of salad leaves or
other leafy green vegetables every day**.

6 You need to get off your backside at least once a day, in a very low-tech, low-effort kind of way. We suggest walking – it's easy, everyone able-bodied can do it, and it doesn't call for any expensive equipment or gym membership. How far and how often you walk initially is up to you – but you need to begin with 10 minutes a day, and walk at a pace that leaves you slightly breathless (but not chronically puffed).

7 We'll just say it again: you really, really need to take your supplements. See *Neris and India's Idiot-Proof Diet*.

8 Embrace fat. Not your own, but good, friendly fats found in delicious butter and good oils. If you like crackling, eat it. Ditto streaky bacon, or mayo, or double cream drizzled (not poured) into vegetable soup. Once again, don't, whatever you do, try to do a low-fat version of this diet, thinking it'll speed things up. It won't. It'll stall you.

9 Weigh yourself once a week, after your morning poo. As the diet progresses and the weight falls off, the temptation to jump on the scales five times a day is overwhelming. Try to resist it. Weight loss is not linear: your weight fluctuates fairly wildly even as you're losing it, and if you suddenly find yourself 2 pounds heavier today than you were yesterday, you'll get depressed – even though it all evens out in the end. So aim for once a week, and ignore the scales, or avoid them altogether, before and during your period.

10 Use a tape measure as well as the scales. You can lose inches off your waist before losing a single pound. Mysterious, but true. Again, don't measure yourself every day. Twice a week, tops.

A note on protein and fat

What happens to the fat you eat? Some will be used in the repair and structure of cell walls throughout the body, and to make vital hormones. Some may be used for energy. The rest is wasted. The fat you eat is broken down into fatty acids in the bowel, by the action of enzymes and bile. These fatty acids are absorbed into the bloodstream and taken to the liver, where they are further processed … into ketones, and into other fatty acid components. Some of the ketones may be used for fuel. Mostly they are excreted in the urine, stool and breath (via the lungs). Unused free fatty acid components are also excreted. Why? Because once fatty acids are broken down into the smaller ketone, acetone and fatty esterols, they cannot be converted back into fat. Without insulin, they cannot be forced into storage in the fat cells. So they are eliminated. This is what Dr Atkins refers to as the 'Metabolic Advantage'.

The other question is: how does eating fat stimulate the burning of body fat? Well, it acts like kindling. It primes the liver into fat-burning and ketone-production mode. Once this ketone production is in full swing, and the dietary fat is used up, the liver starts looking for more sources of fat to process. It turns to your body fat stores, which is what we all want.

CHAPTER THREE

GETTING
ORGANIZED

We can't emphasize this enough: preparation is all. This diet is incredibly easy to follow if your fridge is ready for it, and not so easy if it isn't. If you work long hours, or live miles away from the shops, your new way of eating is going to require forward planning. If you accidentally skip a meal, or eat late, you *will* get hungry on this way of eating, and if there's nothing suitable to hand, you're likely to grab the wrong thing simply because your body is telling you to eat. And that's a big fat disaster.

The following list will help set you up for beginning the diet.

STORE CUPBOARD ESSENTIALS

SAUCES AND OILS

★ Thai fish sauce (nam pla)

★ Sesame oil

★ Olive oil

★ Groundnut oil

★ Tamari soy sauce

★ Wine or cider vinegar

HERBS AND SPICES

★ Curry powder

★ Nutmeg

★ Ground mace

★ Ground cinnamon

★ Thyme

★ Cloves

★ Cardamom pods

★ Cinnamon sticks

★ Cumin seeds

★ Ground cumin

★ Coriander seeds

★ Ground coriander

★ Garam masala

★ Turmeric powder

★ Crushed chillies

★ Paprika

★ Oregano

★ Lemongrass

OTHER

* ★ Mustard powder
* ★ Mustards, including flavoured
* ★ Horseradish
* ★ Baking powder
* ★ Desiccated coconut
* ★ Tomato purée
* ★ Pine nuts
* ★ Ground almonds
* ★ Sesame seeds
* ★ Splenda
* ★ Tahini
* ★ Marigold bouillon powder

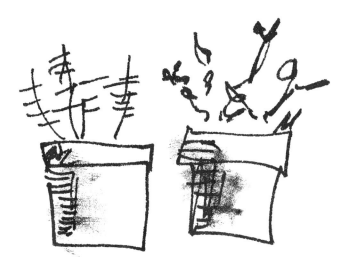

Here is a handy checklist for what you can eat on each phase of the diet. Cut it out, copy it and stick it on your fridge, your cupboards, everywhere you can.

PHASE 1

⋆ Organic, free-range eggs

⋆ Meat. Any kind you like, including roasts, ham, bacon, pastrami, salami, steak, chicken, sausages (posh ones only, please)

⋆ Pâté (the good stuff that comes in slices, not the weird stuff in plastic tubes)

⋆ Fish. Any kind you like, from fresh sea bass to canned tuna

⋆ Olive oil and groundnut oil

⋆ Vinegar. Any kind except balsamic

⋆ Organic, additive-free peanut butter

⋆ Double cream

⋆ Butter

⋆ Herbs and spices

⋆ Sea salt and black pepper

⋆ Nuts. Any kind provided they are au naturel and with no added sugar.

⋆ Vegetables. Any kind excluding potatoes, carrots, corn and peas. The best vegetables for this kind of diet, in general, are green, so any kind of spring greens, spinach, cabbage and so on.

⋆ Avocados

⋆ Lemons and limes

⋆ Tomatoes

⋆ Cheese, any kind from buffalo mozzarella to blue Cheddar, etc.

⋆ Tofu

⋆ Herbal tea

⋆ Unsweetened organic soya milk

PHASE 2

* Non-leafy vegetables – onions, for instance, in increased quantities
* All the berries – blueberries, raspberries, strawberries, etc.
* Cantaloupe and honeydew melon
* Seeds (as well as nuts)
* Dark chocolate, in moderation
* Coconut milk
* Plain yogurt
* Alcohol, clean spirits only, so gin, vodka, rum or whisky with soda water or diet tonic
* Soya flour
* Ground linseed
* Stone-ground, wholewheat bread
* Porridge oats – real ones, not instant

PHASE 3

* Legumes, aka pulses
* Other fruits
* Starchy vegetables
* Whole grains

FRUIT AND VEG YOU CAN EAT

* ★ Any cabbage
* ★ Brussels sprouts
* ★ Salad things
* ★ Pak choi
* ★ Spring greens
* ★ Kale
* ★ Broccoli, but not a whole head at once!
* ★ Cauliflower
* ★ Butternut squash (once or twice a week)
* ★ Aubergines
* ★ Tomatoes in small quantities
* ★ Mushrooms
* ★ All herbs
* ★ Green peppers (not red or yellow)
* ★ Spinach
* ★ Chard, etc.
* ★ Leeks
* ★ Onions in moderation

CHAPTER FOUR

FAQs AND
MENU IDEAS

How big should my portions be?

Try to keep to 'normal' portions, i.e.:

Cheese – the size of a matchbox (not those boxes of cooking matches though!)

Meat/fish – a piece the size of your palm

Salad – enough to fill a standard cereal bowl

Vegetables – a level serving spoon

Cream – a dash or a splash, not a flood

How much water should I drink?

Aim for around 3 litres a day if you can. More, and you may have issues with water retention. Less, and you may be giving your kidneys a hard time.

What protein shake shall I get?

Take a look at what's on offer at your local health food shop and select one with a low carb content. Try to train yourself to like the unflavoured ones and not add too many things to them. A drop of vanilla extract is best, or a teaspoon of peanut butter. Remember to add some double cream for a rich flavour and texture.

Why do I have to give up caffeine and when can I have it again?

Caffeine can stall you. It doesn't happen to everyone, but it is worth giving it up for the first two weeks. After that it's up to you.

When can I drink alcohol again and what can I have?

No alcohol for the initial two weeks, then keep to clear spirits – ideally vodka and soda with a slice of lime. White wine is not really recommended because it is quite carby, but the odd glass won't hurt. That's the odd glass a week, not a night ...

When can I have chocolate?

You can have small amounts of 70% chocolate in Phase 2. Occasionally. That means not every day. And a small amount is not a whole bar.

Why can't I have milk?

Milk contains lactose, which is a sugar. Sugar = carbohydrate.
Cream has far less lactose than milk, which is why it is allowed.

Can I have yoghurt?

Not in Phase 1.

Can I have fizzy water instead of still?

You can have a couple of glasses of fizzy water a day, but no more.

Can I eat crème fraîche?

Yes.

Can I eat Quorn?

It has wheat in it, so we'd prefer you not to eat it.

Can I eat cottage cheese?

Not in Phase 1, but OK in Phase 2.

Can I have fruit teas?

Yes, you can. Experiment – there are some delicious teas out
there. Your local health food shop will have a large selection and
these days most supermarkets sell a good range too.

Can I use Splenda?

You can use Splenda, and it is used in a few of the recipes, usually
as an option, although we don't recommend it as a general rule.
There are two reasons for this: one, because it is chemically
treated sugar which isn't exactly a natural product, and two,
because sugar is incredibly addictive and this plan is designed
to reduce and hopefully stop any sugar/sweet/carbohydrate
addiction. If you continue to have sweetened foods you will never
break that addiction.

How long do I stay on Phase 1?

Our advice is to stay on Phase 1 until you are within a stone or so
of your goal. You can move on to Phase 2 earlier than this if you
wish, but be prepared for the weight loss to slow down.

Why have I stopped losing weight?

It is natural to plateau when on a weight-loss plan. Sometimes your body simply needs to catch up with itself. Make sure that you are sticking religiously to the plan – it is easy to sneak in a little bit here and a little bit there that isn't on the list. The one thing you must get into your head is that cheating is fatal on this WOE (way of eating). You are training your body to process food in a different way, and sneaking in little bits of carbs here and there will only confuse things and stop the weight loss.

Why do I get headaches?

One reason could be your withdrawal from both caffeine and sugar. Another could be dehydration. Don't wait until you are thirsty before drinking water – by the time you feel thirsty you will already be quite dehydrated. Drink your water!

Why is my wee yellow?

The supplements you are taking turn it yellow, especially the B vits.

Why am I feeling moody?

You are dealing with some major issues here. Allow yourself a little slack and remember that it has taken years to grow your fat person, so getting to the slim one will not happen overnight. As you travel on this journey you will find that at various times some challenging thoughts and ideas may jump out and slap you. One of the major aspects of this book has been our attempt to change the way you think about what you eat, when you eat it and how you eat it. Change is often uncomfortable. Try to embrace that feeling, and take the scary steps with your head held high.

On the other hand it could just be that your period is due ...

I do intensive sports – can I have carbs before training?

We have several people on the plan training for a marathon. If you're one of them, it's OK to have carbs (porridge, not 3 rounds of toast and jam) for breakfast. If you're just going to the gym, you should be fine on a protein breakfast – we were.

How do I find out the glycaemic index of foods?

You can look it up online, but we wouldn't bother – everything you need to know about GI is in the diet book and online in the forum.

MENU IDEAS

Here are some daily menu ideas for Phase 1. The asterisks indicate specific recipes in the book.

MENU ONE

BREAKFAST Parma ham and mozzarella
LUNCH Feta cheese, sliced ham, watercress, baby plum tomatoes
EVENING MEAL Celeriac bravas*

MENU TWO

BREAKFAST Indian scrambled eggs*
LUNCH Crab cakes*
EVENING MEAL Thai-style meatballs with peanut sauce*

MENU THREE

BREAKFAST Poached egg and fried mushrooms
LUNCH Butternut and coconut bake*, green salad
EVENING MEAL Tandoori chicken livers with coriander and mint dip*

MENU FOUR

BREAKFAST Bacon and avocado melt*
LUNCH Chicken liver pâté* and celery sticks
EVENING MEAL Moussaka*

MENU FIVE

BREAKFAST Smoked bacon and tomatoes
LUNCH Omelette Gordon Bennett*
EVENING MEAL Butter chicken*, broccoli

MENU SIX

BREAKFAST Butternut bacon and walnuts*

LUNCH Salmon rillettes*

EVENING MEAL Fillet steak in a peppered brandy and cream sauce*, green salad

MENU SEVEN

BREAKFAST Ricotta muffins*

LUNCH Chorizo rapido*

EVENING MEAL Salmon and feta bake*

MENU EIGHT

BREAKFAST Whey protein shake*

LUNCH Cheese and spinach stuffed peppers*

EVENING MEAL Ham, leek and blue cheese pie*

MENU NINE

BREAKFAST Smoked salmon and Boursin rolls

LUNCH Chicken liver salad*

EVENING MEAL Sausage casserole*

MENU TEN

BREAKFAST Egg and sausage muffins*

LUNCH Hot Thai beef salad*

EVENING MEAL Salmon rillettes*, celery sticks

MENU ELEVEN

BREAKFAST Indian scrambled eggs*
LUNCH Lettuce soup with Parma crisps and basil oil*
EVENING MEAL Slow-roast belly pork*

MENU TWELVE

BREAKFAST Spicy sausage and salsa
LUNCH Courgette soup with gingered onions*
EVENING MEAL Slow-roast shoulder of lamb*, cauliflower faux-mash*
and broccoli

MENU THIRTEEN

BREAKFAST Parma ham and mozzarella
LUNCH Feta, olive and butternut salad*
EVENING MEAL Corned beef hash*

MENU FOURTEEN

BREAKFAST Half an avocado with a teaspoon of pecan nut butter
LUNCH Oven-roasted aubergine and tahini salad*
EVENING MEAL Roast cod with herbs and tomatoes*

MENU FIFTEEN

BREAKFAST Smoked salmon, mascarpone and avocado
in gem lettuce leaves
LUNCH Gorgeous grilled mushrooms*
EVENING MEAL Tarragon chicken*, curly kale

MENU SIXTEEN

BREAKFAST Hard-boiled eggs and celery salt
LUNCH Thai Green avocado soup*
EVENING MEAL Keema* with finely shredded cabbage

MENU SEVENTEEN

BREAKFAST Cold cooked sausages and mustard
LUNCH Easy fish pâté* and celery sticks
EVENING MEAL Grilled Portobello mushrooms with
blue cheese dressing*

MENU EIGHTEEN

BREAKFAST Roast ham and cream cheese rolls
LUNCH Quiche and green salad
EVENING MEAL Bee's chilli bake*

MENU NINETEEN

BREAKFAST Half an avocado filled with cream cheese
LUNCH Celeriac dauphinoise*
EVENING MEAL Stir-fried duck with sesame seeds*, spinach

MENU TWENTY

BREAKFAST Ricotta muffins*
LUNCH Kedgeree*
EVENING MEAL Trout with almonds*

MENU TWENTY-ONE

BREAKFAST Indian scrambled eggs*
LUNCH Roast butternut squash soup with Parmesan and bacon*
EVENING MEAL Tagliata with rocket and Parmesan*

MENU TWENTY-TWO

BREAKFAST Parma ham and mozzarella
LUNCH Prawn bhajias*
EVENING MEAL Comforting beef stew*

MENU TWENTY-THREE

BREAKFAST Smoked salmon and Boursin rolls
LUNCH Curried eggs Florentine*
EVENING MEAL Savoury cheesecake*

MENU TWENTY-FOUR

BREAKFAST Salami slices and Brie
LUNCH Spicy egg rolls with tamarind dipping sauce*
EVENING MEAL Fake shepherd's pie*

MENU TWENTY-FIVE

BREAKFAST Whey protein shake*
LUNCH Salade niçoise*
EVENING MEAL Speedy prawn curry*

MENU TWENTY-SIX

BREAKFAST Roasted aubergine and red pepper muffins*
LUNCH Croque monsieur*
EVENING MEAL Paella*

MENU TWENTY-SEVEN

BREAKFAST Hard-boiled eggs and celery salt
LUNCH Crab, green bean and pistachio salad*
EVENING MEAL Pork and olive ravioli*

MENU TWENTY-EIGHT

BREAKFAST Fried sausages

LUNCH Curried cauliflower soup*

EVENING MEAL Chicken with an egg and lemon sauce*, spinach

MENU TWENTY-NINE

BREAKFAST Spicy sausage and salsa

LUNCH Fake pizza*

EVENING MEAL Marinated spiced lamb*, spring greens

MENU THIRTY

BREAKFAST Ricotta muffins*

LUNCH Cauliflower soufflé*

EVENING MEAL Thai salmon fishcakes*, spinach

CHAPTER FIVE

RUBS, OILS, MARINADES AND BUTTERS

For when you can't be arsed to do complicated cooking, but don't necessarily fancy a naked, unadorned lump of meat. These make a massive difference taste-wise, with very little effort on your part.

Eating a lump of protein and some green leafy vegetables can get a little bit monotonous at times, so here are some delicious ideas for sexing up your protein and perking up those veg.

RUBS

Basically a rub is a dry marinade. Make up a batch by mixing all the ingredients together and store in a screw-top jar. To use, massage a couple of tablespoons into your meat or fish. There's no need to do this in advance, although the flavour will be a little more pronounced if you can do it half an hour before cooking.

Cajun spice mix

4 tablespoons paprika
3 tablespoons chilli powder
1 tablespoon mustard powder
1 tablespoon black pepper
1 tablespoon white pepper
1 tablespoon garlic powder
1 tablespoon onion powder
1 tablespoon ground cumin
1 tablespoon dried rosemary
1 tablespoon dried thyme
1 tablespoon dried oregano
1 tablespoon salt

Tandoori rub

2 teaspoons garlic powder
2 teaspoons paprika
1 teaspoon cayenne pepper
1 teaspoon ground coriander
1 teaspoon ground cumin
1 teaspoon ground ginger
¼ teaspoon ground cardamom
¼ teaspoon ground cinnamon
1 teaspoon salt

Citrus rub

2 teaspoons finely grated lemon zest
2 cloves of garlic, crushed
1 teaspoon dried rosemary
½ teaspoon dried thyme
½ teaspoon black pepper
Large pinch of salt

Moroccan-style rub

½ teaspoon cloves
½ teaspoon cumin seeds
½ teaspoon coriander seeds
½ teaspoon fenugreek seeds
½ teaspoon black peppercorns
2 tablespoons paprika
½ teaspoon ground ginger
½ teaspoon ground cardamom
¼ teaspoon ground cinnamon
¼ teaspoon chilli powder
¼ teaspoon ground allspice
1 teaspoon salt

Place the whole spices into a clean coffee grinder and grind to a powder, then mix with the ready-ground spices.

OILS

There are many delicious flavoured oils available in the supermarket. Use them to drizzle over grilled meat or fish for added interest and flavour. Our favourites include chilli, garlic, sesame, avocado and lemon.

MARINADES

Marinades add moisture and flavour, and any acidic ingredient will have a slight tenderizing effect. Whisk everything together, then turn the meat or fish in the marinade and allow to steep in the fridge for anything up to 24 hours.

Basic marinade

100ml oil (olive or groundnut)
Juice and zest of 2 fat lemons
2 cloves of garlic, crushed
1 teaspoon salt
½ teaspoon freshly ground black pepper

Thai-style marinade

100ml groundnut oil
Juice and zest of 2 limes
1 teaspoon fish sauce
1 tablespoon tamari soy sauce
1 tablespoon finely chopped fresh coriander
1 teaspoon easy lemongrass
1 teaspoon easy ginger
1 fresh chilli, finely chopped

Simple herb marinade

100ml oil
1 tablespoon chopped fresh parsley
1 teaspoon chopped fresh rosemary
1 teaspoon chopped fresh thyme
2 tablespoons cider vinegar
½ teaspoon salt

Coconut marinade (fab with prawns or with chunks of fish or chicken)

75g creamed coconut
75ml hot water
2 cloves of garlic
1 or 2 small hot fresh chillies, roughly chopped
1 small onion, peeled and quartered
Grated zest of 1 lime or lemon

Dissolve the creamed coconut in the hot water. Place all the ingredients in a food processor or blender and pulse until you get a paste. Pour over the prawns, fish or chicken and leave for about an hour. Thread the prawns on to skewers and grill or barbecue.

FLAVOURED BUTTERS

These are so easy to make and really perk up a piece of grilled meat or some steamed vegetables.

Pulse 125g of softened butter in a food processor with your chosen flavourings (or mash together with a fork). Once blended, place the butter on a piece of foil, use a couple of forks to squash into a sausage shape, then roll up in the foil and freeze. To serve, add a slice to hot meat, fish or vegetables.

Here are some ideas:

Parsley butter

Add 3 tablespoons of finely chopped fresh parsley and a squeeze of lemon juice.

Coriander butter

Add 1 tablespoon of finely chopped fresh coriander, 1 teaspoon of lime juice, and Tabasco to taste.

Anchovy butter

Add 6 anchovy fillets, the finely grated zest of 1 lemon and a small handful of chopped fresh parsley.

Horseradish butter

Add 2 teaspoons of hot horseradish sauce.

Roquefort butter

Add 125g of Roquefort cheese to the butter and mash together with a fork.

Olive butter

Add 1 tablespoon of black olive tapenade and a squeeze of lemon juice.

Basil butter

Add a large handful of fresh basil leaves and 2 peeled cloves of garlic.

Mint butter

Add a large handful of fresh mint leaves and 1 teaspoon of cider vinegar.

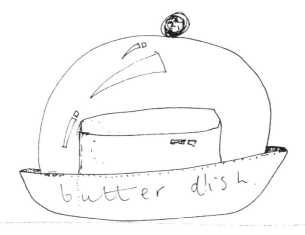

butter dish.

CHAPTER SIX
BREAKFASTS

As we were saying in the introduction, many people who follow a low-carb diet find breakfast a little on the challenging side. Not many people have the time to cook themselves elaborate things first thing in the morning, plus what your stomach does and doesn't find acceptable at 7.30 a.m. varies from person to person. Here are some suggestions which should satisfy even the most jaded, egged-out palate.

QUICK BREAKFASTS

As in, things to eat on the hoof.

★ Hard-boiled eggs and celery salt
★ Egg mayonnaise
★ Stuffed eggs
★ Scotch eggs
★ Salami slices
★ Spicy sausage
★ Spicy sausage and salsa
★ Roast ham and cream cheese rolls
★ Roast ham and mustard mayonnaise rolls
★ Parma ham and Taleggio cheese rolls
★ Parma ham and mozzarella cheese
★ Onion bhajias
★ Small packet of nuts
★ Celery and cream cheese
★ Celery and peanut butter
★ Celery and pâté
★ Celery and blue cheese dip
★ Roast beef and horseradish mayonnaise rolls
★ Cheese portions
★ Cheese cubes and pickled onions
★ Smoked salmon and Boursin rolls
★ Roast chicken and pesto mayonnaise
★ Aubergine and feta cheese rolls
★ Frittata wedges
★ Crustless quiche wedges
★ Cold cooked sausages and mustard

- ★ Sausage and bacon rolls
- ★ Crispy bacon strips and egg mayonnaise
- ★ Feta cheese and tapenade
- ★ King prawns and mayonnaise
- ★ King prawns and salsa
- ★ Dressed crab
- ★ Smoked mackerel and horseradish mayonnaise
- ★ Cold Thai-style meatballs and peanut dip
- ★ Cold meatballs and mustard mayonnaise
- ★ Any cold curry and a spoon
- ★ Half an avocado
- ★ Half an avocado filled with cream cheese
- ★ Half an avocado filled with pecan nut butter
- ★ Tinned mackerel in tomato sauce with chopped raw onion

SERVES 1
1 scoop of whey protein powder
1 glass of unsweetened soya milk

Flavouring of your choice (vanilla
essence, peanut butter, nuts,
double cream)

WHEY PROTEIN SHAKE

1 Whiz it all up (you can do this with a fork – it doesn't go all lumpy) and drink.

4 slices of streaky bacon
1 ripe avocado, halved, stone removed
1 tablespoon salsa

50g good melting cheese (Taleggio,
Cheddar, Stilton, Gruyère)
2 tablespoons double cream

BACON AND AVOCADO MELT

1 Preheat the grill.

2 Cook the bacon until crisp, then snip into pieces with scissors.

3 Put half the ingredients into each avocado half in this order –
salsa, bacon, cheese, cream.

4 Place on a grill pan and put on the lowest shelf. Grill until the
top is brown and bubbling.

SERVES 2

1 small onion, peeled and very finely sliced
Oil for frying
50g freshly grated Parmesan cheese
4 tablespoons cream cheese or
    mascarpone cheese

4 cherry tomatoes, quartered
½ a green pepper, finely diced
4 slices of corned beef (from the deli
    counter rather than the stuff in a tin)

CORNED BEEF CANNELLONI

1 Preheat the oven to 180°C/gas mark 4.

2 Fry the onion in a little oil until tender.

3 Mix together the onion, Parmesan, cream cheese, tomatoes
and pepper. Spread a quarter of the mixture on to the short
end of each slice of corned beef, then carefully roll up into a
cigar shape.

4 Place on a non-stick baking sheet and bake in the oven for
20 minutes.

SERVES 1

1 egg, separated
A dash of cream
2 heaped tablespoons cauliflower
   faux-mash (see page 214)

A sprinkling of freshly grated nutmeg
2 large field mushrooms, stalks removed
1 tablespoon freshly grated Parmesan cheese

CAULIFLOWER STUFFED MUSHROOMS

1 Preheat the oven to 200°C/gas mark 6.

2 Mix the egg yolk, cream, cauliflower and nutmeg together thoroughly.

3 Whisk the egg white until stiff and fold into the cauliflower mixture.

4 Spoon this mixture on to the mushrooms, sprinkle over the grated Parmesan and bake in the oven until risen and golden brown.

▶ Chopped ham, crumbled bacon or flaked buttery kippers could be added to the stuffing mixture if desired.

SERVES 1
½ a small butternut squash   6 walnut halves, roughly chopped
4 slices of smoked streaky bacon   1 tablespoon sherry vinegar

BUTTERNUT, BACON AND WALNUTS

1 Preheat the oven to 190°C/gas mark 5.

2 Remove the seeds from the butternut squash, brush with oil and bake until tender.

3 While the squash is baking, snip the bacon into small pieces and fry in a non-stick pan until crisp. Add the walnut pieces to the pan and fry for about 30 seconds. Add the sherry vinegar and allow to boil, then turn off the heat.

4 Take the squash out of the oven and put on to a serving plate. Use a fork to mash the flesh within the shell, then spoon over the bacon and walnuts.

A knob of butter

A little groundnut oil

8 sausages

1 onion, finely sliced

A bunch of fresh herbs (thyme is nice, but any fresh herbs would do)

PERFECT FRIED SAUSAGES

1 Put the butter and a dot of groundnut oil into a frying pan and get it nice and hot. Add the sausages. Now turn the heat down to the minimum and leave them alone for at least 20 minutes. Then turn them over and repeat on the other side. The result is a really regal sausage, sticky and caramelized on the outside and cooked properly within.

2 While the sausages are cooking, if you can be bothered, fry the onions on a very gentle heat in some butter until they've gone brown at the edges; toss in the herbs and a little liquid – leftover stock, leftover gravy, a corner of a stock cube, or even just water, and simmer the whole thing until it's all melted and melded together. Eat the onions with the sausages.

SERVES 1

Butter and groundnut oil for frying
1 small onion, very thinly sliced
2 eggs
A small handful of chopped fresh
   coriander

1 fresh green chilli (less if you fear
   heat), chopped
1 tomato, chopped
A pinch of ground cumin
A pinch of ground coriander
Salt and freshly ground black pepper

INDIAN SCRAMBLED EGGS

1 Melt some butter with a drop of oil. The smaller the pan, the less contact with direct heat, and the fluffier the eggs will be.

2 When hot, add the onion slices and fry until coloured and crispy around the edges.

3 Meanwhile, mix all the remaining ingredients in a bowl. Tip into the pan containing the onions and scramble for a couple of minutes, or until set.

40g ground flaxseed

60g walnut pieces

50g finely ground almonds

2 teaspoons ground cinnamon

1/4 teaspoon sea salt

4 tablespoons Splenda

4 large eggs

240ml unsweetened soya milk

1 teaspoon baking powder

Groundnut oil for frying

FAUX WAFFLES/PANCAKES

★ Phase 2 only

You can get ground flaxseed (aka linseed) from your friends at the health food shop. If you try to do it yourself in a coffee grinder or blender, it won't be fine enough. Flaxseeds are very good, because of their high omega-3 content.

1 Blend the flaxseed, walnuts, almonds, cinnamon, salt and Splenda in a food processor until the walnuts are finely ground.

2 In a bowl, whisk the eggs and half the soya milk. Add the walnut mixture and combine well. Cover and refrigerate for at least an hour, or overnight (but no longer).

3 When you're ready to eat, add the baking powder and the remaining milk, and stir well.

4 Heat an oil-greased frying pan and drop blobs of the mixture on to it. This makes US-style fat pancakes, not crêpes. Cook for about 2 minutes or until browned, then flip. You can eat them slathered with butter, and you could also add vanilla extract to the batter.

MAKES 12
2 red onions, sliced
Oil for frying
100g feta cheese, crumbled

Leaves from 3 sprigs of fresh thyme
12 eggs
120ml double cream
120ml water

FETA AND RED ONION MUFFINS

1 Preheat the oven to 190°C/gas mark 5 and oil a 12-cup muffin tray.

2 Fry the onions in a little oil until soft, then divide the onions, cheese and thyme leaves between the muffin cups.

3 Whisk together the eggs, cream and water and pour over the cheese and onion.

4 Bake for 30 minutes on the top shelf, until golden. Allow the muffins to cool slightly before attempting to remove them from the tray.

½ a small butternut squash, cubed
Oil and butter for frying
6 fresh sage leaves, chopped

100g wedge of Brie cheese, chopped
12 eggs
120ml double cream
120ml water

BUTTERNUT, BRIE
AND SAGE MUFFINS

1 Preheat the oven to 190°C/gas mark 5 and oil a 12-cup muffin tray.

2 Fry the butternut squash in a little oil and butter until tender. Add the sage leaves for the last couple of minutes. Divide the squash and chopped Brie between the muffin cups.

3 Whisk together the eggs, cream and water and pour over the squash and Brie.

4 Bake for 30 minutes on the top shelf, until golden. Allow the muffins to cool slightly before attempting to remove them from the tray.

MAKES 12

150g cooked smoked haddock
1 teaspoon cumin seeds, dry-roasted in
   a small non-stick pan, then crushed

A small handful of fresh coriander leaves
12 eggs
120ml double cream
120ml water

SMOKED HADDOCK MUFFINS

1 Preheat the oven to 190°C/gas mark 5 and oil a 12-cup muffin tray.

2 Flake the smoked haddock, removing any skin, and divide between the muffin cups. Sprinkle over the crushed cumin seeds and add few coriander leaves to each cup.

3 Whisk together the eggs, cream and water and pour over the smoked haddock.

4 Bake for 30 minutes on the top shelf, until golden. Allow the muffins to cool slightly before attempting to remove them from the tray.

1 large aubergine, cut into 1cm dice
1 red pepper, cut into 1cm dice
2 tablespoons oil
2 cloves of garlic, crushed

100g Fontina, Taleggio or other
   melting cheese, cubed
12 eggs
120ml double cream
120ml water

ROASTED AUBERGINE AND RED PEPPER MUFFINS

1 Preheat the oven to 190°C/gas mark 5 and oil a 12-cup muffin tray.

2 Put the aubergine and red pepper into a bowl, add the oil and mix to coat. Spread out on a baking tray and cook in the oven until softened and slightly blackened at the edges here and there.

3 Divide the aubergine, pepper, garlic and cheese between the muffin cups.

4 Whisk together the eggs, cream and water and pour over the vegetables and cheese.

5 Bake for 30 minutes on the top shelf, until golden. Allow the muffins to cool slightly before attempting to remove them from the tray.

MAKES 12
100g raw tiger prawns
A small handful of fresh coriander leaves

200ml coconut cream
1 teaspoon Thai green curry paste
12 eggs

SPICY TIGER PRAWNS AND COCONUT CREAM MUFFINS

1 Preheat the oven to 190°C/gas mark 5 and oil a 12-cup muffin tray.

2 Chop the prawns, divide between the muffin cups and add a few coriander leaves to each cup.

3 Whisk together the coconut cream and the green curry paste, then whisk in the eggs. Pour this mixture over the prawns and coriander leaves.

4 Bake for 30 minutes on the top shelf until golden. Allow the muffins to cool slightly before attempting to remove them from the tray.

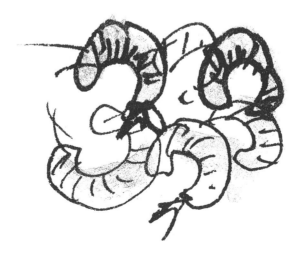

455g sausages

Groundnut oil

1 medium-sized onion, sliced (optional)

12 eggs

120ml double cream

120ml water

Sea salt

170g grated Cheddar cheese

EGG AND SAUSAGE MUFFINS

1 Preheat the oven to 180°C/gas mark 4 and oil a 12-cup muffin tray.

2 Remove the sausages from their skins and fry in a little oil until browned (with onions if you like; they're nice caramelized). Divide the sausage meat equally between the muffin cups.

3 Whisk together the eggs, cream, water and salt. Pour over the sausage meat and top with the cheese.

4 Bake for 20 minutes on the top shelf until golden and fluffy. Allow the muffins to cool slightly before attempting to remove them from the tray.

MAKES 4

2 cloves of garlic, crushed
2 teaspoons olive oil
1 tablespoon pine nuts

100g baby spinach leaves
250g ricotta cheese
1 egg, beaten
2 tablespoons chopped fresh chives

BAKED RICOTTA MUFFINS

1 Preheat the oven to 200°C/gas mark 6 and oil a 4-cup muffin tray.

2 Fry the garlic in the oil until brown/fragrant, and add the pine nuts (but don't turn your back for a minute, or they'll burn!). Add the spinach, stir until wilted, and leave to cool.

3 Combine the spinach mixture in a bowl with the cheese, egg and chives, then divide between the muffin cups.

4 Bake for about 15 minutes (check after 10 minutes), until puffed and brown. Allow the muffins to cool slightly before attempting to remove them from the tray.

1 small punnet of blueberries
1 small punnet of raspberries
12 eggs

120ml double cream
100ml water
2 tablespoons Splenda
½ teaspoon vanilla extract

MIXED BERRY MUFFINS

⋆ Phase 2 only

1 Preheat the oven to 190°C/gas mark 5 and oil a 12-cup muffin tray.
2 Divide the berries between the muffin cups.
3 Whisk together the eggs, cream, water, Splenda and vanilla extract and pour over the berries.
4 Bake for 30 minutes on the top shelf, until golden. Allow the muffins to cool slightly before attempting to remove them from the tray.

CHAPTER SEVEN

LUNCHES AND LIGHT MEALS

These are for when you're not really in the mood to don a pinny and come over all domestic goddess. They're quick, they're snappy, they're utterly delicious, but you can throw them together quickly with minimal effort.

Neris did her first year on the diet using 'assembled' food like this. You don't have to spend hours in the kitchen to stick to the diet.

Obviously, you don't have to have them for lunch: all the recipes here would make a lovely supper. Or breakfast, if you're that way inclined.

QUICK OFFICE LUNCH IDEAS

An old-fashioned sandwich shop, of the kind that has sandwich fillings laid out in boxes behind a glass counter, has lots to offer for lunch ideas. If you should be lucky enough to be in striking distance of such a gem, cherish it and make friends with the staff. Have a recce, and then choose from any of the following breadless options. Have generous dollops of any of the following:

* Prawn mayonnaise
* Egg mayonnaise
* Tuna mayonnaise
* Crispy bacon
* Sliced tomato
* Sliced cucumber
* Sliced avocado
* Sliced olives
* Smoked salmon
* Cream cheese
* Any other kind of cheese – mozzarella is nice with tomato and avocado
* Roast beef (and you can have horseradish with it)
* Roast pork, lamb, etc.
* Hams
* Any fish
* Salamis and other cold meats
* Sausages
* Pâté
* Taramasalata, if it's not bulked out with bread (ask)

Ask for any of these ingredients in salad form, i.e. with lettuce and dressing (check for sugar), have the salad on the side and use the lettuce to make wraps. It's not necessarily wildly exciting, but then neither is it significantly more boring than the usual lunchtime sarnie, frankly.

SERVES 2

230g crabmeat, brown and white
230g cooked white fish, skinned, boned and flaked
1 tablespoon finely chopped fresh parsley
1 tablespoon each finely diced green and red pepper

2 rounded tablespoons mayonnaise
2 eggs, beaten
1 teaspoon baking powder
1 tablespoon Worcestershire sauce
1 heaped teaspoon Cajun seasoning
Oil and butter for frying

CRAB CAKES

1 Mix together all the ingredients except the oil and butter. Chill in the fridge for at least an hour.

2 Using a spoon, scoop up the mixture and form into cake shapes as best you can – the mixture is quite sloppy. They will firm up somewhat as they cook.

3 Heat the oil and butter in a non-stick frying pan and fry the cakes gently on both sides until firm and golden brown.

4 These are lovely served with lemon wedges and mayonnaise mixed with some wholegrain mustard.

▸ In Phase 2/3, coat the crab cakes in soya flour before frying.

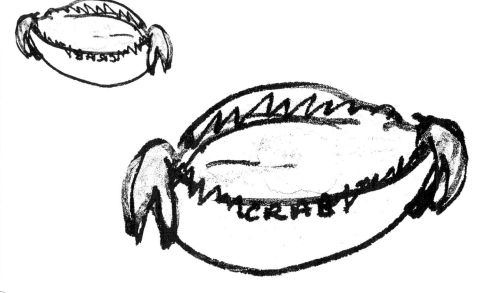

SERVES 4
200g spinach
6 hard-boiled eggs
1 small onion, finely sliced
1 tablespoon oil

1 tablespoon curry powder*
300ml double cream
1 tablespoon desiccated coconut
50g grated Parmesan and Cheddar
    cheese, mixed

CURRIED EGGS FLORENTINE

1 Preheat the oven to 180°C/gas mark 4.

2 Put the spinach in a colander and pour over a kettle of boiling water (sometimes you need to do this twice to wilt it). Use a saucer to press down on the spinach and drain off as much water as possible, then tip the spinach on to a chopping board and chop finely with a sharp knife.

3 Spread the spinach over the bottom of a shallow ovenproof dish. Halve the eggs and place cut side down on top of the spinach.

4 Fry the onion slowly in the oil until caramelized and golden brown. Stir in the curry powder and fry for about a minute, then pour in the cream, bring to the boil and simmer gently until the sauce has thickened. Stir in the coconut and spoon the sauce evenly over the eggs.

5 Top with the grated cheese and bake until golden and bubbling.

★ You don't have to use ready-made curry powder – make your own spice mix if you prefer. Get experimenting!

250g raw king prawns
1 teaspoon easy ginger
1 teaspoon easy garlic
1 teaspoon garam masala
Juice of 1 lemon
150g ground almonds
1 teaspoon nigella seeds (black onion seeds)

1 fat fresh green chilli, finely chopped
  (seeds removed if you prefer)
1 teaspoon baking powder
1 tablespoon chopped fresh coriander
1 egg
100ml double cream
Groundnut oil for frying

PRAWN BHAJIAS

1 Chop the prawns roughly and mix together with the ginger, garlic, garam masala and lemon juice. Allow to marinate in the fridge for an hour.

2 Mix together the ground almonds, nigella seeds, chilli, baking powder, coriander and egg and add enough double cream to make a thick batter. Beat well. Stir the batter into the prawns.

3 Heat a thin film of oil in a non-stick sauté pan over a low heat. When the oil is hot, use a dessertspoon to dollop the mixture into the pan. Leave the bhajias alone for at least 3 minutes to allow a crust to form – they are very fragile.

4 Use a spatula to turn the bhajias over and cook for another 3 minutes, or until they are firm and golden brown on both sides.

MAKES 25

1 teaspoon cumin seeds
200g ground almonds
½ teaspoon turmeric
1 teaspoon salt
½ teaspoon baking powder
2 fresh green chillies, finely chopped
   (seeds removed if you prefer)

4 eggs, separated
100ml double cream
3 medium onions, cut in half and very
   finely sliced
Groundnut oil for frying
Chopped fresh coriander and mint to serve

ONION BHAJIAS

1 Roast the cumin seeds in a dry, medium hot pan until they start to smell fragrant. Remove from the heat and allow to cool.

2 Mix together the ground almonds, cumin seeds, turmeric, salt, baking powder and chopped chillies.

3 Beat in the egg yolks and cream.

4 Whisk the egg whites to soft peaks and fold into the almond mixture.

5 Separate the onion slices and gently fold into the almond batter a third at a time until all the onion is incorporated.

6 Cover the bottom of a frying pan with groundnut oil to about 0.5cm depth and put over a low to medium heat.

7 Using a dessertspoon, scoop up spoonfuls of the batter and fry on both sides until deep brown and crisp.

8 Serve hot and sizzling straight from the pan, sprinkled with chopped fresh coriander and mint.

1 recipe quantity of cheesy garlic bread, made up to the end of step 3 (see page 92)
A large knob of butter
2 tablespoons cream cheese

40g grated cheese – preferably Gruyère, but strong Cheddar is fine
1 tablespoon mustard
4 thin slices of good-quality ham
Groundnut oil for frying

CROQUE MONSIEUR

1 Using the largest pastry cutter you have, stamp out as many rounds as you can from the bread, then carefully cut each round in half horizontally through the middle. Butter each one and lay butter side down on a board.

2 Mix together the cream cheese, grated cheese and mustard and spread on one half of the sandwich. Top with sliced ham and cover with the other half of the sandwich, butter side out. Press together as firmly as you can.

3 Heat a small splash of oil in a frying pan and fry gently over a low heat until golden on both sides and the filling is hot.

▸ In Phase 2/3 you could make this with thinly sliced wholemeal bread.

SERVES 6
230g chicken livers
115g butter
A couple of fresh sage leaves
150ml double cream

CHICKEN LIVER PÂTÉ

1 Wash the livers and snip off any dodgy-looking bits. Chicken livers look a bit dodgy anyway, so don't get carried away – anything vaguely green-looking is not good, and any sinews or fatty bits should go. Otherwise, have faith.

2 Heat 30g of the butter in a small frying pan and fry the livers until browned but still soft inside. If you press one with your finger it should feel about as firm as the end of your nose.

3 Lift the livers out of the pan with a slotted spoon and put into a food processor, then chuck the sage leaves into the frying pan and sizzle for a few seconds. Scrape any butter and the sage into the food processor too.

4 Blitz, scrape down the sides and blitz again. Add enough of the double cream to make the mixture soft and floppy. Scrape into a bowl, level the top and allow to cool.

5 Heat the rest of the butter very gently in a small pan and when it separates into liquid butter and solids, carefully pour the clear liquid butter over the top of the pâté.

6 Refrigerate until needed.

▸ In Phase 2/3 you could add a splash of brandy after the sage leaves and allow it to bubble before putting it into the food processor.

Oil for frying
3 spring onions, chopped
1 fresh red chilli, finely sliced

A knob of butter
3 eggs, lightly beaten
75g spicy cured chorizo sausage
50g Gruyère cheese, grated

OMELETTE GORDON BENNETT

1 Heat a teaspoon of oil in a small non-stick frying pan.
Add the spring onions and chilli and fry until the onions have
softened slightly. Remove with a slotted spoon.
Wipe the pan out with kitchen paper and add another splash
of oil and the butter.

2 Once the butter has stopped foaming, add the eggs. As the egg
sets in the pan, lift it with a fork and allow the uncooked egg to
run underneath. Work the fork around the pan, creating a
jumble of cooked egg towards the middle as you go. Once you
have almost no liquid egg left, leave the omelette to set. As it is
setting, pile the onion mixture and the chopped chorizo into
the middle and add the grated cheese.

3 Use a spatula to flip the omelette in half and then on to a plate.

▸ In Phase 2 add a chopped red pepper. In Phase 3 add a sliced
cold boiled potato.

SERVES 2
150g smoked fish
150g full-fat cream cheese
Juice of 1 lemon (more if you like
    it sharper)
½ teaspoon paprika

EASY FISH PÂTÉ

Not really a recipe, it's so simple. Also, pleasingly 70s.

1 Get any kind of smoked fish – mackerel, smoked salmon, smoked trout – or any tinned fish you fancy (e.g. tuna). Stick it in a blender with the cream cheese, lemon juice and paprika. Blend.
2 Serve with crisp lettuce leaves or cucumber sticks to eat it off.

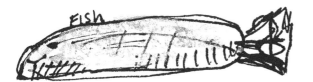

SERVES 1 GREEDY ARTICLE
OR 2 WITH A SALAD

A splash of olive oil
60g butter
1 onion, halved and finely sliced
1 small cauliflower, trimmed and grated
120ml stock (you can use Marigold
   bouillon powder)

1 rounded dessertspoon curry powder
115g naturally smoked haddock, poached
   and flaked
2 tablespoons double cream
2 hard-boiled eggs (optional)
2 tablespoons chopped fresh parsley

KEDGEREE

*If you like smoked haddock, this is delicious. It would also work
with kipper fillets or cooked chicken and some prawns.*

1 Heat the oil in a deep frying pan and add the butter. When the
butter has stopped foaming, add the onion and fry briskly until
the edges are turning brown.

2 Tip in the cauliflower and stir around for a couple of minutes
to coat in the butter and oil. Add the stock and the curry powder
and simmer for another couple of minutes, until the cauliflower
is tender and the stock has all but disappeared.

3 Gently stir in the flaked fish, then the cream.

4 Shell the eggs and cut into quarters.

5 Serve the kedgeree garnished with the eggs and sprinkled with
chopped parsley.

▶ In Phase 3 add some cooked lentils.

SERVES 4–6

BASE	FILLING
100g hazelnuts	3 large eggs
150g ground almonds	140ml double cream
125g butter	150g grated cheese

BASIC QUICHE

1 Preheat the oven to 180°C/gas mark 4.

2 Base line a 24cm springform tin with baking parchment.
Put the hazelnuts in a dry frying pan and heat gently until they
change colour and go a slightly darker brown. You might hear a
faint sizzling too. Put them straight into a food processor and
whiz to the size of digestive biscuit crumbs.

3 Pour the nuts into a bowl, and add the ground almonds and a
pinch of salt. Melt the butter, then pour it over the nuts and mix
thoroughly to combine. Tip the mixture into the base-lined tin
and spread out gently with the back of a spoon, trying to get it
evenly covered across the base and up the sides – the sides are
resistant to this but do the best you can, pressing firmly with the
back of the spoon to pack it down as evenly as possible. Put it
into the fridge for about half an hour to set.

4 Beat the eggs into the cream. Scatter the cheese evenly over the
base, then pour in the eggs and cream and bake in the oven for
35 minutes on the middle shelf.

5 To this basic mix you can add whatever you like: ham, smoked
salmon, crispy bacon, prawns, chopped-up sausages, oven-
roasted veggies … the list is endless.

▸ In Phase 2/3 add some porridge oats to the crust.

MAKES 12
EGG ROLLS
4 eggs, beaten
50ml water
2 fresh red or green chillies, finely chopped
A handful of fresh coriander, finely chopped
A small handful of chives, chopped
Salt and freshly ground black pepper
Groundnut oil for frying
1 small pack of stir-fry vegetables

125g cooked king prawns or sliced chicken breast
2 tablespoons tamari soy sauce
DIPPING SAUCE
1 tablespoon tamarind pulp*
50ml water
1 teaspoon Splenda
1 teaspoon easy ginger
1 teaspoon easy garlic or 1 clove of garlic, crushed
1/4 teaspoon crushed dried chillies (optional)
1 tablespoon tamari soy sauce

SPICY EGG ROLLS WITH TAMARIND DIPPING SAUCE

1 Mix together the eggs, water, chillies, coriander, chives, salt and pepper in a jug.

2 Heat a small non-stick frying pan and use some kitchen paper to wipe the inside of the pan with a little groundnut oil.

3 Pour in enough of the egg mixture to give a thin even covering of the base. Allow to set. Then loosen the edges with a spatula and remove to a plate. Cook all the egg mixture in this way.

4 Add a little more oil to the pan and fry the vegetables until almost cooked but still crisp. Add the prawns or chicken and the tamari and heat through.

5 Put a spoonful of the mixture on to a pancake and roll up.

6 To make the dipping sauce, just mix all ingredients together and allow the flavours to mingle for an hour before serving.

*Tamarind pulp can be obtained by soaking a lump of dried tamarind in hot water then rubbing the pulp through a sieve, leaving the seeds behind. (Or by just buying a jar from Bart Spices ...)

SERVES 3
½ a cauliflower
2 large eggs
A splash of cream

1 tablespoon chopped fresh parsley
About 6 gratings of nutmeg
A large handful of grated Cheddar
cheese

CAULIFLOWER SOUFFLÉ

1 Preheat the oven to 180°C/gas mark 4.
2 Steam the cauliflower until very tender, then mash thoroughly.
Stir in the eggs, cream, parsley, nutmeg and Cheddar.
3 Scrape into a small Pyrex casserole dish and bake until puffed
up and golden brown.

▸ This will work with other cooked vegetables too: spinach,
broccoli, butternut squash, etc.

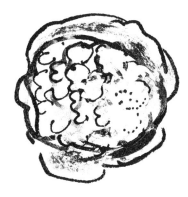

SERVES 1
½ a medium celeriac
A bowl of water with a squeeze of
lemon juice
1 small onion

Olive oil and butter for frying
Salt and freshly ground black pepper
350ml double cream
100ml soya milk (or water)
50g Parmesan cheese

CELERIAC DAUPHINOISE

1 Preheat the oven to 180°C/gas mark 4.

2 Cut the celeriac into four pieces, peel them, and cut each slice into pieces about the thickness of a pound coin. Slice straight into the bowl of water to prevent the celeriac going brown.

3 Peel and finely slice the onion and fry gently in oil and butter until golden brown. This can take up to 20 minutes – the trick is to do it slowly until the onions are almost melting.

4 Put a layer of celeriac into the bottom of a small lasagne type dish and sprinkle with a little of the onion and a little salt and pepper. Repeat with another layer, and so on, finishing with celeriac.

5 Let down the double cream with enough soya milk (or water) to make the consistency of single cream. Pour over the dish until the liquid almost reaches the top. Sprinkle with lots of Parmesan.

6 Bake for approximately 45 minutes, until bubbling and golden and the celeriac is tender when poked with the point of a knife.

SERVES 4
250g salmon fillet
50g butter
1/2 tablespoon very finely chopped
   fresh parsley

1/4 teaspoon powdered mace
Lemon wedges
Salad leaves

SALMON RILLETTES

1 Wash the salmon fillet in cold water and run your fingers across the surface to check for any stray bones. If you find any, pull them out with eyebrow tweezers.

2 Place the salmon in a shallow Pyrex dish and cover with clingfilm. Cook in a microwave on medium heat for approximately 3 minutes – the fish should flake easily, but take care not to overcook it. If after 3 minutes it isn't cooked, put it back for 30 seconds at a time until done. The flesh should be just opaque at the thickest part. Allow to cool, then flake with a couple of forks.

3 Melt the butter with the parsley and mace in a small saucepan or in the microwave, and stir through the flaked salmon. Pack into ramekins and level the tops with the back of a spoon. Cover with clingfilm and chill thoroughly. Serve with lemon wedges and salad leaves.

115g cream cheese, at room temperature
4 large organic eggs, beaten
80ml double cream
30g grated Parmesan cheese
1 tablespoon chopped fresh chives
½ teaspoon chopped garlic
½ teaspoon dried oregano

100g grated cheese of your choice
230g fresh mozzarella cheese
120ml tomato passata
145g sliced mushrooms, sautéd in a little olive oil
2 sausages, casings removed, crumbled and pan-fried

FAKE PIZZA

1 Preheat the oven to 180°C/gas mark 4. Butter or oil a shallow baking dish, approximately 33 x 22cm.

2 Blend the cream cheese until smooth, then add the eggs little by little, beating until fully incorporated. Add the cream, Parmesan, chives, garlic and oregano. Blend until smooth. Scatter the cheese of your choice plus half the mozzarella in the baking dish. Pour the egg mixture over the cheese and bake for 30 minutes.

3 Spread the 'base' with tomato sauce. Scatter the mushrooms and sausage over the top (or ham, if preferred, or bacon). Cover with the remaining mozzarella and grill until brown.

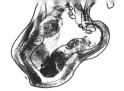

SERVES 2

1 large or 2 small fresh red peppers	A pinch of mixed spice
100g frozen spinach	100g cottage cheese
1 egg	50g feta cheese
4 fresh sage leaves, finely chopped	2 tablespoons Parmesan cheese

CHEESE AND SPINACH STUFFED PEPPERS

1 Preheat the oven to 200°C/gas mark 6.

2 Cut the peppers in half lengthways, keeping the stalks on. Remove the seeds and wash the pepper halves. Line them up like little bowls.

3 Defrost the spinach and squeeze to remove excess water.

4 Beat the egg in a bowl with the sage and mixed spice. Add all the other ingredients and mix roughly together, keeping the mixture lumpy. Spoon into the pepper halves.

5 Arrange on a baking tray and bake in the oven for 25 minutes.

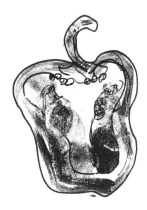
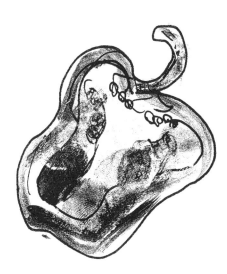

MAKES ABOUT 6 PORTIONS

300g ground almonds
1 teaspoon salt
1 teaspoon baking powder
4 eggs
4 tablespoons olive oil

2 tablespoons groundnut oil
3 (or more!) garlic cloves, peeled and
    crushed
75g softened butter
A handful of fresh parsley, chopped
100g mozzarella cheese, cubed

CHEESY GARLIC BREAD

*Although this is Phase 1 friendly, it does still contain carbs, so don't
eat a whole one ... or only once in a blue moon.*

1 Preheat the oven to 180°C/gas mark 4.

2 Mix together the ground almonds, salt and baking powder.
Beat in the eggs and oils, using a wooden spoon. If the mixture
is a bit stiff, beat in some water a tablespoon at a time until the
mixture drops off the spoon easily when you tap it on the side
of the dish (known as 'dropping consistency').

3 Divide the mixture between two 20cm non-stick oiled cake tins
and level the tops. Bake for 20 minutes. Remove from the oven,
loosen in the tin and turn on to a cooling rack.

4 Mix together the garlic, butter and parsley.

5 Place one disc on a large piece of tin foil and spread with the
garlic butter. Scatter over the mozzarella and place the other
disc on top. Wrap with foil.

6 Return to the oven for another 10–15 minutes until piping hot
and the cheese has melted.

▶ Leave out the cheese and add some grated lemon zest if you
prefer. Or use a different type of cheese – Gorgonzola would
be fab. Chopped fresh rosemary would be nice added to the
batter too.

SERVES 2–4

½ a very large butternut squash (about 600g)   A pinch of salt
1 teaspoon korma curry powder   1 tin of coconut milk

BUTTERNUT AND COCONUT BAKE

★ Phase 2/3 only

1 Preheat the oven to 180°C/gas mark 4.

2 Peel the squash and cut into 1cm dice. Put into a saucepan, cover with boiling water and simmer for 3 minutes. Drain the squash, put it into a shallow ovenproof dish and sprinkle over the curry powder and a little salt.

3 Pour the coconut milk into the pan and heat through until all the lumps have gone and it is coming to the boil. Pour over the squash.

4 Bake in the oven for 20–30 minutes, until brown and bubbling.

▸ In Phase 3 add a tin of chickpeas.

A piece of Parmesan (and a bit
    of Cheddar too, if you like)
A pinch of cayenne pepper

PARMESAN CRISPS

*Not really a lunch, or a light meal, but perfect if you're craving
something crunchy like crisps or biscuits. Which you will, at some
point.*

1 Preheat the oven to 190°C/gas mark 5.
Cover a baking sheet with baking parchment or those clever
silicone non-stick sheets (good investment, plus they last
forever).

2 Coarsely grate the Parmesan or Cheddar, or a mixture of the
two. Add a pinch of cayenne to the pile if you like a bit of heat
to your crunch.

3 Pile the cheese on to the baking sheet in little clusters.
Obviously they are going to spread as they melt, so make sure
you space them far apart.

4 Stick them in the oven and watch them like a hawk – they only
take a few minutes.

5 Allow the crisps to cool and peel off. If they've melted into one
big sheet, break it apart.

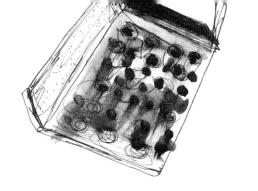

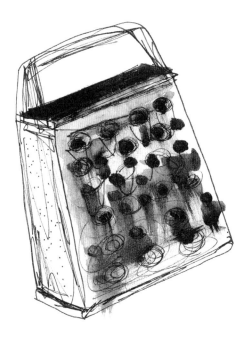

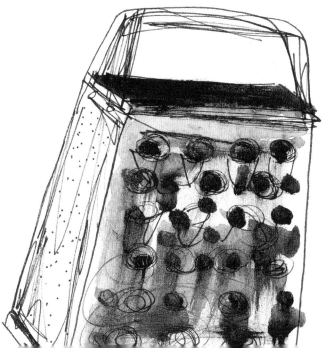

CHAPTER EIGHT
TAKE FIVES

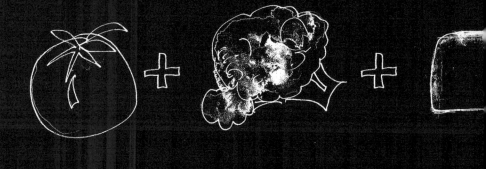

Totally genius, this section, which was Bee's idea. For when you're in a hurry and can't be doing with going to the shops with some great massive list of ingredients, but still want something extremely delicious to eat. Each recipe serves 1 person.

Note: when you have very few ingredients, it's important to make sure that they are of the highest possible quality.

CREAMY BEANY CHICKEN

SERVES 1
1 chicken breast
50g French beans
4 cherry tomatoes
½ teaspoon crushed chillies
120ml double cream

Slice the chicken breast into thin strips. Top and tail the beans and cut into thirds. Halve the cherry tomatoes. Fry the chicken strips until opaque, add the beans and crushed chillies and continue frying until the beans are beginning to soften. Stir in the cream and bring to the boil. Add the tomato halves and serve immediately.

CHORIZO RAPIDO

SERVES 1
1 fennel bulb
1 small onion
½ a red pepper
50g chorizo sausage
50g Manchego cheese

Slice the fennel, onion and red pepper. Fry in a little oil and butter until softened and golden. Cut the chorizo into chunks and add to the pan. Stir and fry until the sausage is heated through. Sprinkle over the cubed Manchego and allow it to melt in the heat of the pan.

CRAB ROYALE

SERVES 1
1 dressed crab in the shell
1 tablespoon double cream
15g finely chopped fresh parsley
2 splashes Tabasco
1 tablespoon grated Parmesan cheese

Remove the crab meat from the shell and mix with the cream, parsley and Tabasco. Pile back into the shell and sprinkle with the Parmesan. Place under a hot grill until golden brown and bubbling.

CHICKEN LIVER SALAD

SERVES 1
100g chicken livers
4 slices of streaky bacon
12 small button mushrooms
2 tablespoons red wine vinegar
watercress to serve

Wash and trim the chicken livers, chop the streaky bacon and wipe the mushrooms with a piece of kitchen towel. Fry the bacon in a little oil until it begins to release its fat, then add the livers and the mushrooms and continue frying briskly until the livers are brown all over and feel just firm to the touch. Add the red wine vinegar and boil briskly for 30 seconds. Serve with watercress.

GORGEOUS GRILLED MUSHROOMS

SERVES 1
1 large field mushroom
30g crumbly goat's cheese
1 tablespoon chopped walnuts
1 tablespoon chopped fresh parsley
1/2 teaspoon green peppercorns

Remove the stalk from the mushroom. Place the mushroom cap stalk side down on a grill pan and brush with oil. Place under a hot grill for 2 minutes, then turn it stalk side up. Mix together the cheese, walnuts, parsley and peppercorns and spoon into the mushroom cap. Grill for 3 minutes, until the top is golden brown.

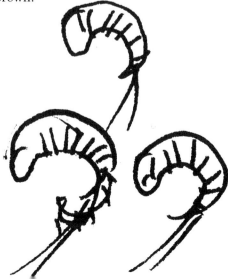

MASCARPONE HASH

SERVES 1

1 small leek
1 courgette
a handful of chopped fresh parsley
a little leftover cooked meat
80g mascarpone cheese

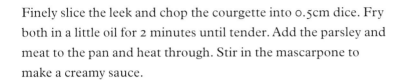

Finely slice the leek and chop the courgette into 0.5cm dice. Fry both in a little oil for 2 minutes until tender. Add the parsley and meat to the pan and heat through. Stir in the mascarpone to make a creamy sauce.

▶ This is a moveable feast – if using cold lamb, substitute mint for the parsley. Cooked turkey would be brilliant with some sliced sprouts instead of courgette, smoked pork loin and shredded cabbage … you get the picture. The amount of meat isn't important, even a few leftover shreds will add depth and flavour to the dish.

SPEEDY PRAWN CURRY

SERVES 1

300g chopped tomatoes
5 nuggets of frozen spinach
1 heaped teaspoon curry powder
2 tablespoons desiccated coconut
200g prawns (defrosted if frozen)

Put the tomatoes into a sieve and drain off most of the liquid. Put into a small saucepan with the spinach, curry powder and desiccated coconut and slowly bring to the boil. Simmer gently for 5 minutes, until the spinach has defrosted and the sauce is thick. Turn off the heat, add the prawns and allow to stand for 1 minute before serving.

CHAMPAGNE SALMON

SERVES 1
100g boneless skinless salmon fillet
6 asparagus spears
50g butter
15g snipped chives
50ml champagne

Put the salmon fillet into a shallow Pyrex dish and cover with clingfilm. Microwave on full power for 2 minutes, then check. You want the fish just barely cooked in the middle (it will carry on cooking slightly), so put it back for 30 seconds at a time until it's cooked. Rub the asparagus with a little oil and griddle until tender. Melt the butter in a small saucepan, add the chopped chives and any juices from the salmon, then using a small 'magic' whisk beat in the champagne to make the sauce. Serve with the salmon and asparagus.

SMOKY FRITTATA

SERVES 1
2 eggs
2 tablespoons double cream
1 large hot-smoked fish fillet (salmon, mackerel, kipper)
15g snipped fresh chives
3 heaped tablespoons grated Parmesan cheese

Whisk the eggs and cream together and flake the fish from any skin (check for stray bones). Heat a knob of butter in a small non-stick frying pan. Pour the egg mixture into the pan and scatter over the flaked fish and the chives. When almost set, sprinkle with the Parmesan and put the pan under a preheated grill until the top has set and the cheese is brown. Serve hot or cold.

AVOCADO IN A WARM DRESSING

SERVES 1
1 avocado
4 slices of streaky bacon, cut into small strips
1 tablespoon pine nuts
20ml sherry/cider vinegar
30g crumbled Stilton cheese

Peel and slice the avocado. Put the bacon into a non-stick frying pan and cook until crisp, then scatter it over the avocado. Add the pine nuts to the fat in the pan and fry until golden. Pour in the vinegar and allow to come to the boil, then quickly scrape any sticky bits off the bottom of the pan. Pour this over the bacon and avocado and top with the crumbled Stilton.

PIQUANT LAMB CHOPS

SERVES 1
3 fat lamb chops
1 teaspoon tapenade
1 teaspoon tomato purée
roughly chopped fresh parsley
finely grated zest of 1 lemon

Grill the lamb chops under a hot grill until the fat is golden and crisp. Spread the tomato purée and then the tapenade over the top of the chops and grill for another 30 seconds. Sprinkle with parsley and lemon zest before serving.

CHAPTER NINE
SOUPS

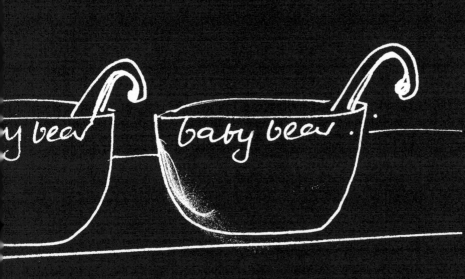

Easy-peasy, warming, cosy and wintry (or brisk and summery, in some cases) – plus, soups practically make themselves. And they're a brilliant way of getting vegetables down you without really noticing.

SERVES 2
1 butternut squash
Olive oil for brushing
500–750ml vegetable or chicken stock
    (cubes are fine, Marigold bouillon   2 tablespoons grated Parmesan cheese
    powder is better)   4 rashers of crispy bacon

ROAST BUTTERNUT SQUASH SOUP WITH PARMESAN AND BACON

1 Preheat the oven to 190°C/gas mark 5.

2 Cut the butternut squash in half lengthways. Brush it with olive oil, place it on a baking tray, and stick it in the oven for an hour or so, depending on its size – it's ready when it's soft.

3 Scoop out the flesh and whiz it in a blender. Put it into a pan with enough vegetable or chicken stock to achieve a consistency that's pleasing to you. Gently heat through for 20 minutes or so. Serve with 1 big heaped tablespoon of Parmesan per bowl, and some crispy, crumbled bacon.

▸ If you want to gild the lily, you could add some rosemary leaves to the roasting squash, and/or drizzle the finished product with a little truffle oil.

8 slices of Parma ham

A large bunch of fresh basil, tough
   stalks removed

120ml mild olive oil or groundnut oil

50g butter

2 tablespoons olive oil

1 leek, cleaned and finely sliced

4 flat lettuces (the soft floppy 'old-
   fashioned' type of lettuce), washed
   and roughly chopped

¼ teaspoon ground mace

500ml vegetable or chicken stock

LETTUCE SOUP WITH PARMA CRISPS AND BASIL OIL

1 Preheat the oven to 230°C/gas mark 8.

2 Place the Parma ham slices on a non-stick baking sheet and bake in the oven until browned – this doesn't take very long, so keep a watchful eye on them. Allow to cool; they will crisp up as they do. If you want to show off, 'zig-zag' the slices on to oiled skewers before baking to make frilly crisps ...

3 Put the basil and the 120ml of oil into a blender or a 'thunderstick' goblet. Blend thoroughly to a purée. Line a small sieve or tea-strainer with kitchen paper and place over a bowl. Tip in the contents of the blender and leave to filter through the paper.

4 In a large saucepan heat the butter and the 2 tablespoons of olive oil and fry the sliced leek gently until softened but not coloured.

5 Add the lettuce and stir around for a couple of minutes until coated with the oil and butter. Stir in the mace. Put a lid on the pan (or cover tightly with foil) and turn the heat to the lowest possible setting on the smallest ring for 10 minutes or until fully wilted.

6 Add the stock and bring to a simmer. Cook for another 5 minutes, then blend to a smooth velvety consistency. Serve drizzled with the basil oil and with the Parma ham crisps alongside.

SERVES 4

2 ripe avocados
230ml double cream
2 tablespoons unsweetened
    desiccated coconut

700ml vegetable or chicken stock
1 tablespoon Thai green paste
Lime wedges and fresh coriander
    leaves to serve

THAI GREEN AVOCADO SOUP

1 Halve the avocados, remove the stones and, using a spoon, scrape the flesh into a food processor. Blitz to a purée with a little of the cream.

2 Spread the coconut on a baking sheet and grill until golden. Keep a close eye on it – it burns very easily.

3 Put the remaining cream, the stock and the Thai green paste into a pan and heat to simmering point, then whisk in the avocado purée. Do not allow it to boil.

4 Serve with lime wedges on the side, and garnished with the toasted coconut and coriander leaves.

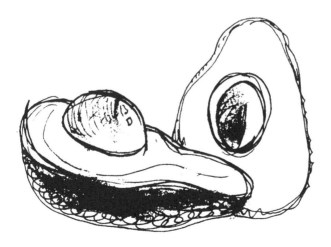

SERVES 4

1 medium onion, peeled, cut in half and
  very finely sliced
oil for frying
1 small courgette, cut into small batons
A 1cm piece of fresh ginger, peeled and
  finely grated

50g butter
1 medium onion, peeled and finely chopped
2 cloves of garlic, peeled and chopped
1kg courgettes, roughly chopped
1 litre vegetable or chicken stock
200ml double cream
Salt and freshly ground black pepper

COURGETTE SOUP WITH GINGERED ONIONS

1 Fry the finely sliced onion in a little oil until pale golden brown, then add the courgette batons and the grated ginger and continue frying until the onions are deep golden brown and the courgettes are tender. Put to one side and allow to cool.

2 Melt the butter in a large saucepan and fry the chopped onion and the garlic until they are both softened and golden. Add the chopped courgettes and continue cooking over a low heat for 10 minutes, stirring occasionally.

3 Add the stock and bring to the boil. Simmer for a further 10–15 minutes.

4 Remove from the heat and allow to cool slightly. Using a hand blender, liquidizer or food processor, blitz until smooth.

5 Stir in the cream and add a little more stock or water if the soup is too thick. Add salt and pepper, put back on the heat and stir until hot, but not boiling.

6 Serve with the gingered onions and courgette batons.

SERVES 4
1 medium leek, cleaned and thinly sliced
Oil and butter for frying
1 tablespoon curry powder

1 litre vegetable or chicken stock
1kg bag of frozen cauliflower florets
A dash of double cream
A few fresh coriander leaves

CURRIED CAULIFLOWER SOUP

1 Fry the leeks gently in a little oil and butter until softened.

2 Add the curry powder and cook for about 30 seconds.

3 Add the stock and cauliflower and bring to the boil, then reduce the heat and simmer until the cauliflower is tender.

4 Using a stick blender, food processor or blender, whiz the soup to a purée.

5 Serve with a swirl of double cream and float a few coriander leaves on top.

SERVES 4
1 medium onion, diced
Oil and butter for frying
1 litre vegetable or chicken stock

500g frozen spinach
100ml double cream
Salt and ground black pepper
Freshly grated nutmeg

SPINACH SOUP

1 Fry the onion in the oil and butter until softened and pale gold.

2 Add the stock and spinach and bring to the boil. Simmer for
5 minutes.

3 Use a 'thunderstick', blender or food processor to whiz to
a smooth purée.

4 Add the double cream, then salt, pepper and nutmeg to taste.
If the soup is very thick, add a little more stock and bring back
to a simmer before serving.

SERVES 4

4–6 dried ceps (using a few dried mushrooms in this soup really boosts the flavour)

A splash of oil

50g butter

1 medium onion, diced

250g mushrooms

1 litre vegetable or chicken stock

1 teaspoon dried tarragon

30ml dry sherry (optional)

Salt and freshly ground black pepper

Double cream or flavoured butter (see page 48)

MUSHROOM SOUP

1 Soak the ceps in a little hot water for 20 minutes. Then strain off the liquid and reserve.

2 Heat the oil and butter and fry the onion until starting to brown. Add the mushrooms and stir to coat in the oil and butter – there may not be enough to coat all the mushrooms, but don't worry. Using the smallest heat source and the lowest possible setting, cover the pan and leave on the heat for 15 minutes.

3 Remove the lid and add the stock, soaked dried mushrooms, tarragon, sherry (if using) and strained dried mushroom liquid. Stir well, then bring to the boil and simmer for 10 minutes.

4 Puree with a 'thunderstick', blender or food processor and taste. Adjust the seasoning.

5 To serve, drizzle with a swirl of double cream or float a slice of flavoured butter on top of each serving.

SERVES 4

4 medium onions, peeled and thickly sliced
1 litre well-flavoured stock (it's definitely
    worth saving a couple of chicken
    carcasses in the freezer to make the
    stock for this; the quality of the stock
    makes all the difference)

Leaves from 4 fresh thyme sprigs
50ml brandy
Olive oil
1 recipe quantity of cheesy garlic bread,
    made up to the end of step 3 (see page 92)
A couple of handfuls of grated Gruyère
    cheese

OVEN-ROASTED ONION SOUP

⋆ Phase 2

1 Preheat the oven to 190°C/gas mark 5.

2 Brush the onion slices with olive oil and lay out in a single layer on a baking sheet. Roast in the oven until lightly charred at the edges, turning over to brown both sides.

3 Bring the stock to the boil, then add the onions and thyme leaves and simmer for 15 minutes.

4 Add the brandy and simmer for another 5 minutes.

5 Meanwhile stamp out rounds of bread (one round per serving), brush with olive oil and toast or fry.

6 Ladle the soup into heatproof bowls, float a bread round on each and top with a large heap of grated Gruyère. Place the bowls on a grill pan and put under a hot grill until the cheese is bubbling.

▸ Eat with care – there is nothing quite like the pain of a blisteringly hot slice of onion slapping you on the chin.

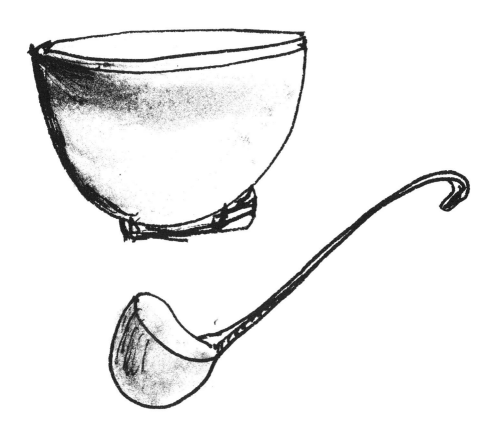

CHAPTER TEN

SALADS

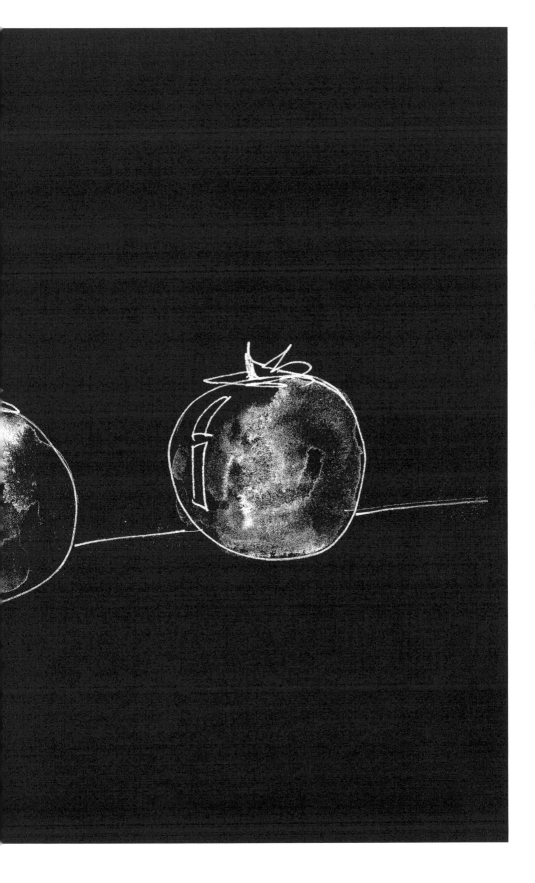

Salads. Hmm. We weren't mad keen, because we've always thought of salads as being unattractively diet-foody, as in the kind of food you might feed your rabbit. These are the precise opposite of those kinds of salads. They have heft. They have balls. They are man-salads, and they won't leave you mooching around the kitchen wondering what else you can eat.

SERVES 1 AS A MAIN, 4 AS A SIDE
A 2.5cm slice of butternut squash,
  peeled and cut into small dice
1 tablespoon olive oil
½ teaspoon Cajun spice mix or similar
  (plain chilli powder would do)

A handful of rocket leaves
A handful of baby spinach leaves
100g feta cheese, crumbled
8 black olives (stoned)
2 tablespoons pine nuts, toasted
Vinaigrette (see page 209)

FETA, OLIVE AND BUTTERNUT SALAD

1 Preheat the oven to 190°C/gas mark 5.

2 Put the diced squash into a bowl and add the oil. Mix to coat, then spread on a non-stick baking tray and bake in the oven until golden brown and tender.

3 Remove from the oven and sprinkle with the Cajun spice mix. Mix the salad leaves, feta and olives in a shallow bowl, and sprinkle over the squash and pine nuts.

4 Drizzle with a little vinaigrette.

3 tablespoons tamari soy sauce

3 tablespoons groundnut oil

2 tablespoons fish sauce (nam pla)

Juice of 2 limes

1 x 100g steak (sirloin, fillet), sliced across the grain as thinly as possible

A 2.5cm piece of fresh ginger, peeled and grated

1 teaspoon Splenda

2 cloves of garlic, smashed

2 or 3 fresh red chillies (the thin ones are best), finely sliced

50ml stock, made with Marigold bouillon powder

Oil for frying

25g creamed coconut, grated

Flat-leaf lettuce leaves, torn into pieces

Cos lettuce leaves, torn into pieces

2 spring onions, sliced

15g fresh coriander, chopped

HOT THAI BEEF SALAD

1 Whisk together 1 tablespoon each of tamari, groundnut oil, fish sauce and lime juice. Pour the mixture over the sliced steak, squish it around in the liquid and leave to marinate for an hour or so.

2 To make the dressing, put the remaining tamari, oil and fish sauce into a bowl and whisk in 2 tablespoons of lime juice, the ginger, sweetener, garlic, chillies and Marigold stock.

3 Pour a dash of oil into a frying pan over a medium high heat. When the oil is hot, add the sliced beef and stir-fry briskly until the outside of the meat is browned.

4 Pour over the dressing and when it boils (it takes seconds), stir in the creamed coconut.

5 Serve the beef on top of the lettuce leaves, sprinkled with sliced spring onions and chopped fresh coriander.

SERVES 2 AS A MAIN, 4 AS A SIDE

1 large aubergine (about 500g)

6 shallots

1 head of garlic

Olive oil

50g pine nuts (toasted if preferred)

15g fresh flat-leaf parsley, finely
 chopped

TAHINI DRESSING

2 tablespoons tahini

2 tablespoons water

1 tablespoon olive oil

Juice of ½ a lemon

A dash of cream

OVEN-ROASTED AUBERGINE
AND TAHINI SALAD

1 Preheat the oven to 220°C/gas mark 7.

2 Using a little 'magic' whisk, combine the tahini and water until smooth. Add the oil, then the lemon and finally stir in the cream. Season to taste and set aside until you need it.

3 Cut the aubergine into chunks. Peel and halve the shallots. Separate the garlic cloves but don't peel them. Put everything into a large mixing bowl and drizzle with plenty of olive oil. Stir and mix (easiest with your hands) until everything is well coated, then spread out on a solid roasting tray.

4 Put into the oven until everything is soft and lightly charred at the edges.

5 Tip on to a serving platter, popping the garlic cloves from their skins as you do so.

6 Drizzle with the tahini dressing and scatter over the pine nuts and parsley.

7 Serve at room temperature.

SERVES 2

100g trimmed green beans
2 tablespoons olive oil
½ a small red onion, finely diced
50g shelled pistachios, chopped
1 fresh green chilli, finely sliced (seeds
   removed if you prefer)

1 clove of garlic, finely chopped
Salt and freshly ground black pepper
115g fresh crabmeat – brown and white
Juice of 1 lemon
3 tablespoons finely chopped fresh parsley

CRAB, GREEN BEAN AND PISTACHIO SALAD

1 Cook the green beans in lightly salted boiling water until cooked, but still retaining some 'bite'. Drain and put into a bowl.

2 Heat the oil in a shallow pan and fry the onion briefly. Add the pistachios, chilli and garlic and fry briefly until the garlic just starts to change colour. Pour the contents of the pan over the green beans, season with salt and pepper and mix together.

3 Toss in the crabmeat. Squeeze over the lemon juice and sprinkle with chopped parsley.

SERVES 2
Juice of 1 lemon
1/2 a celeriac, peeled, sliced and cut
   into thin matchsticks
1 tablespoon Dijon mustard
3 tablespoons mayonnaise

1 tablespoon chopped fresh parsley
2 fat gherkins, finely diced
1 tablespoon capers, rinsed and chopped
   (optional)
50g piece of Napoli salami, diced
Salt and freshly ground black pepper

CELERIAC AND SALAMI REMOULADE

1 Squeeze the lemon juice over the celeriac and mix with your hands.

2 Add the rest of the ingredients, mix together thoroughly, and chill for 30 minutes before serving.

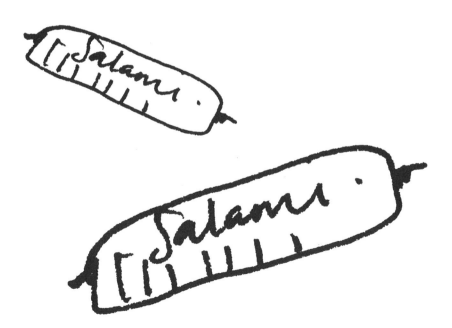

SERVES 2
250g samphire*
A knob of butter
1 small onion, finely diced

100ml dry white wine
1kg mussels, cleaned
Zest and juice of 1 lemon
Zest and juice of 1 lime

SAMPHIRE AND MUSSEL SALAD

1 Plunge the samphire into boiling water for 1 minute. Refresh under cold running water, then drain thoroughly.

2 Melt the butter in a large pan and gently cook the onion until soft. Turn up the heat, pour in the wine and when it starts to boil vigorously tip in the mussels and clap on the pan lid. After a couple of minutes, shake the pan, then check to see if the mussels have opened. If not, put the lid back on and check again after another couple of minutes.

3 Remove the mussels from the pan with a slotted spoon. Take the meat out of the shells if you prefer, and mix with the samphire.

4 Add the lemon and lime juice and zest to the juices in the pan and bring to the boil. Cook until the sauce has reduced and becomes syrupy, then spoon over the salad.

* If you can't get samphire, slender asparagus stalks would make a good substitute.

SERVES 2
200g salmon fillet
1 tablespoon tandoori paste
1 tablespoon mayonnaise
Juice of 1 lemon

100g mangetout peas
4 spring onions, trimmed and chopped
50ml vinaigrette (see page 209)
1 tablespoon finely chopped fresh mint
   leaves

TANDOORI SALMON AND MANGETOUT SALAD

1 Run your fingers over the salmon fillet and remove any stray bones. Cut into chunky cubes.

2 Mix together the tandoori paste, mayonnaise and lemon juice. Add the salmon cubes and turn in the mixture to coat.

3 Steam the mangetout for 2 minutes or until barely tender, then place in a sieve and refresh under cold running water. Drain thoroughly. Stack 2 or 3 mangetout at a time, slice into four lengthways, and pile the slices into a dish with the spring onions.

4 Thread the salmon on to skewers and cook under a hot grill for about 10 minutes, turning once or twice.

5 Mix together the vinaigrette and the finely chopped fresh mint leaves and stir through the vegetables.

6 Serve the vegetables with the salmon on top.

SERVES 6 AS A STARTER, OR AS AN ACCOMPANIMENT TO SOMETHING ELSE

1 head of romaine lettuce, rinsed, dried and chopped
1 red onion, thinly sliced
1 handful of pitted black olives
1 green pepper, chopped
1/2 a red pepper, chopped
2 large tomatoes, chopped
1 cucumber, sliced
200g crumbled feta cheese
6 tablespoons olive oil
1 teaspoon dried oregano
Juice of 1 lemon
Freshly ground black pepper

GREEK SALAD

1 In a large salad bowl, combine the lettuce, onion, olives, green and red peppers, tomatoes, cucumber and cheese.

2 Whisk together the olive oil, oregano, lemon juice and plenty of black pepper. Pour this dressing over the salad, toss and eat.

SERVES 1

Salad leaves of your choice
½ a tomato, chopped up small
1 tin of tuna in olive oil
A handful of cooked green beans

2 hard-boiled eggs, each cut into
   4 or 6 crescents
A handful of fresh flat-leaf parsley leaves
Sea salt and freshly ground black pepper
Vinaigrette (see page 209)

SALADE NIÇOISE

1 Jumble everything together.

2 Eat.

SALADS ARE NICE

CHAPTER ELEVEN

MAIN COURSES

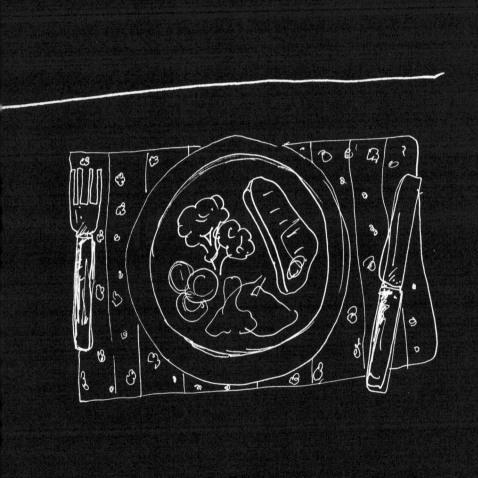

Big fat family-sized dinners for people with appetites. There's nothing here that we wouldn't feed our skinny little friends – the recipes are delicious and will do you proud, diet or no diet.

SERVES 4

½ a medium butternut squash, peeled and cubed
1 small egg, beaten
2 smoked mackerel fillets

1 tablespoon chopped fresh parsley
A splash of olive oil
A knob of butter
Lemon wedges to serve

SMOKED MACKEREL FISHCAKES

1 Steam the squash until just tender, and mash roughly. Leave to cool for 5 minutes, then mix in the egg.

2 Flake the mackerel and fork through the mash, along with the parsley.

3 Line a baking tray with silicon paper. Form the mixture into cakes, place on a plate or small baking tray, and refrigerate for an hour.

4 Heat the oil in a shallow frying pan and add the butter. When it stops foaming, use a fish slice to carefully place the fishcakes in the pan (they are quite fragile, so treat them gently).

5 Leave them alone for at least 3 minutes (to allow a crust to form), then turn them over carefully and brown the other side.

6 Serve with lemon wedges.

▸ In Phase 2 coat the fishcakes in medium oatmeal before frying.

SERVES 2

4 medium courgettes, cut in half
   lengthways
1 small onion, finely chopped
2 cloves of garlic, peeled and finely
   chopped
Olive oil for frying

A knob of butter
50g feta cheese
1 tablespoon pine nuts
8 fresh mint leaves, chopped
50g Stilton cheese
1 slice of good smoked ham, chopped
1 large egg, beaten

COURGETTES WITH TWO STUFFINGS

1 Preheat the oven to 190°C/gas mark 5.

2 Simmer the courgettes in salted boiling water for 4 minutes, then drain. Hold the courgettes in a clean tea towel and, using a teaspoon, scrape the seedy middles out of each half. Chop the middles and set aside. Turn the halves upside down to drain on some kitchen paper or the clean tea towel for 10 minutes.

3 Fry the onion and garlic in a splash of olive oil and the butter until golden. Add the chopped courgette middles and fry for another couple of minutes. Split the onion mixture evenly between two small mixing bowls.

4 Into one bowl crumble the feta, and add the pine nuts and mint.

5 Into the other crumble the Stilton and mix in the chopped ham.

6 Add half the beaten egg to each bowl and mix in thoroughly. Stuff four of the courgette halves with one mixture and four with the other. Put the stuffed courgettes into a small baking dish which will hold them snugly. Drizzle with olive oil and bake until golden and bubbling.

7 Serve with a crisp green salad.

▸ Phase 3 or non IPDers could add a little apricot chutney to the Stilton filling.

SERVES 2–4

1 celeriac, peeled and cut into 2.5cm cubes
Olive oil for frying
5 tablespoons olive oil
1 small onion, finely sliced
1 fresh red chilli, finely chopped (more if
     you like)

2 smashed cloves of garlic
1 tin of chopped tomatoes
1 tablespoon tomato purée
1 tablespoon wine or cider vinegar
1 teaspoon paprika
Salt

CELERIAC BRAVAS

1 Shallow fry the celeriac in hot oil until golden all over. Transfer to a serving dish.

2 Heat the 5 tablespoons of oil and add the onion. Fry until golden. Add the chilli and garlic and fry for another minute. Stir in the tinned tomatoes, tomato purée, vinegar and paprika and reduce for 5 minutes. Season with a little salt. Pour the sauce over the celeriac, or serve separately with the celeriac alongside.

3 This is best served warm, not hot.

250g chicken livers (defrosted if frozen) 2 tablespoons double cream
1 tablespoon tandoori spice mix 1 quantity vinaigrette (see page 209)
1 tablespoon olive oil 15g fresh coriander, finely chopped
25g butter 15g fresh mint, finely chopped

TANDOORI CHICKEN LIVERS WITH CORIANDER AND MINT DIP

1 Rinse the chicken livers in a sieve and look for any dodgy bits –
don't get too carried away, as they look pretty dodgy to start
with. Tip them into a bowl and sprinkle over the tandoori spice
mix. Stir the livers around to make sure they are all coated, then
put into the fridge for an hour.

2 Heat the oil and butter in a frying pan and fry the livers until
just cooked. They should feel about as firm as the end of your
nose. Remove from the pan with a slotted spoon.

3 Whisk the cream into the vinaigrette, and stir in the
chopped herbs.

4 Serve the livers with cocktail sticks on the side for dipping.

SERVES 2
5 tablespoons olive oil
1 tablespoon cider vinegar
Juice and zest of 1 lemon
Juice and zest of 1 lime

1 teaspoon black peppercorns, crushed
2 thick fresh tuna steaks (about
   200g each)
1 small onion
1 green pepper

TUNA KEBABS WITH BLACK PEPPER AND CITRUS VINAIGRETTE

1 To make the dressing, whisk together the olive oil, cider vinegar and citrus juices. Stir in the lemon and lime zest and the crushed peppercorns and set aside for about an hour.

2 Cut the tuna steaks into 2cm cubes.

3 Quarter the onion and separate into layers.

4 Remove the seeds and stalk from the pepper and cut into 2cm squares.

5 Using the largest pieces of onion, thread the tuna, onion and pepper pieces on to metal skewers. Brush with oil, then grill or barbecue until the tuna is barely cooked through – it will be ruined if it is overcooked.

6 Pour the dressing over the kebabs immediately and serve.

▶ If preferred, blanch the onion and pepper squares in boiling water for 1 minute to soften them before threading them on the skewers.

1 tablespoon sesame seeds

1 tablespoon groundnut oil

2 duck breast fillets, skin removed, cut into chunks

1 fat fresh red chilli, seeds removed, finely chopped

2 cloves of garlic, finely sliced

A 1cm piece of fresh ginger, peeled and finely sliced

1 small head of broccoli, separated into tiny florets

$1/2$ teaspoon five-spice powder

1 tablespoon fish sauce (nam pla)

1 tablespoon tamari soy sauce

100ml water

1 tablespoon sesame oil

STIR-FRIED DUCK*
WITH SESAME SEEDS

1 Toast the sesame seeds in a dry pan until fragrant, brown and sizzling slightly. Put to one side.

2 Heat the oil in a wok and add the duck meat. Stir and fry until the meat is beginning to brown and loses its raw look, then add the chilli, garlic and ginger and continue frying for another minute or so.

3 Add the broccoli and stir in the five-spice powder, fish sauce, tamari and water. Bring to a brisk boil, then reduce the heat and simmer until the broccoli is bright green and tender and most of the liquid has evaporated.

4 Garnish with the toasted sesame seeds and sesame oil before serving.

* This works nicely with pheasant or pork fillet too.

SERVES 2
2 whole trout or 4 trout fillets
1 tablespoon olive or groundnut oil

25g butter
75g sliced almonds
100ml double cream

TROUT WITH ALMONDS

1 Fry the trout in a little oil and butter – 3 minutes on each side if using whole trout, 1 minute on each side if using fillets. Remove from the pan and keep warm.

2 Add the almonds to the pan and fry gently until they brown, watching them like a hawk – they burn in an instant.

3 As soon as the almonds are ready, pour in the cream and shake the pan until heated through.

4 Serve the trout with the sauce spooned over.

3 leeks, outer layer, roots and coarse
   green tops removed
1 tablespoon olive or groundnut oil
10g butter

120ml water
1/2 teaspoon Marigold bouillon powder
140ml double cream
70g blue cheese

BLUE CHEESY LEEKS

This goes brilliantly with roast meat, especially lamb, or just eat it on its own with a large spoon.

1 Check the leeks for dirt by splitting them to about halfway down and fanning out the leaves. Rinse under the tap, then cut into 0.5cm slices.

2 Heat the oil and melt the butter until it foams. Add the leeks and stir-fry until they are beginning to turn golden at the edges.

3 Add the water and the Marigold powder. Stir until the powder dissolves, then bring to a simmer and cook until the stock reduces slightly and becomes syrupy.

4 Stir in the double cream and allow to bubble for about a minute until the sauce thickens.

5 Stir in the cheese, turn off the heat and allow the cheese to meld with the sauce.

▸ For a one-pot meal, this is nice with some chopped walnuts added and some crispy bacon crumbled over the top.

SERVES 2

500g lamb mince
1 onion, chopped
2 cloves of garlic, crushed
2 teaspoon dried oregano
1 teaspoon ground cinnamon
2 tablespoon tomato purée

100ml water
1 large aubergine
Olive or groundnut oil
3 eggs
300ml double cream
200g feta cheese

MOUSSAKA

1 Preheat the oven to 180°C/gas mark 4.

2 Fry the lamb mince, breaking any lumps up with a fork or wooden spoon, until starting to brown. Drain off any excess fat, then add the onion and garlic and continue frying until the onion has softened.

3 Stir in the oregano, cinnamon, tomato purée and water. Bring to a simmer, then cover and cook for 20 minutes over a low heat.

4 Slice the aubergine, brush with oil, and grill, fry or griddle until softened but not mushy. It should be golden coloured.

5 Stir the meat, and if it still looks a bit too liquid, simmer with the lid off for 5 minutes or so.

6 Beat together the eggs and cream and stir in the crumbled feta.

7 Layer the aubergine over the meat and pour the feta custard over the top.

8 Bake in the oven for approximately 45 minutes, or until the top is golden brown.

100g chopped walnuts
150g ground almonds
125g grated Parmesan cheese
1 teaspoon dried thyme
125g butter
300g Philadelphia cheese

250g mascarpone cheese
250g crumbly white cheese
 (e.g. Lancashire, feta, Cheshire)
150ml double cream
6 eggs, separated
Salt
1 teaspoon mustard powder

SAVOURY CHEESECAKE

1 Preheat the oven to 160°C/gas mark 3.

2 Put the nuts, Parmesan and dried thyme in a bowl. Melt the butter and pour it into the bowl, mixing thoroughly. Tip into a base-lined 23cm spring-form tin and spread out gently with the back of a spoon, trying to get the base evenly covered. Once spread out, press the mixture down firmly with the back of the spoon so that you pack it down as evenly as possible. Put into the fridge for about half an hour to set.

3 Put all the cheeses into a food processor and pulse until smooth. Scrape into a large mixing bowl and add the cream, egg yolks, a pinch of salt and the mustard powder. Using a hand mixer, beat again until smooth and creamy.

4 Wash and dry the beaters thoroughly and put the egg whites into a large mixing bowl. Whisk until they form stiff peaks. To test this, stop the beaters and lift them out of the mixture – when it stays up in pointy peaks you know it has been whisked enough.

5 Take a large metal spoon and stir a third of the egg white into the cheese mixture to loosen it. Gently fold in the other two-thirds until no streaks of egg white can be seen.

6 Pour the topping into the tin and level with the back of a spoon.

7 Bake in the oven for 1¼–1½ hours, until the top is bronzed and when lightly pressed feels slightly wobbly but not floppy. Turn off the oven and leave to cool for 1 hour (it will sink quite a bit).

8 Open the door and leave for another hour, then chill thoroughly overnight in the fridge.

9 As with the sweet version (see page 193), it is slightly tricky to cut, so use a sharp knife and a cake slice. Don't be surprised if once again the first slice is a bit of a bugger to get out.

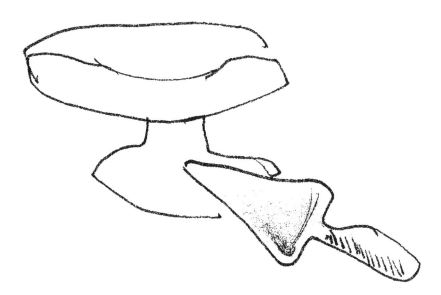

½ teaspoon saffron
100ml hot chicken stock
Olive oil for frying
8 skinless chicken thighs
1 Spanish onion, cut into wedges
125g chorizo sausage, cut into chunks
2 cloves of garlic, peeled and chopped

A 400g tin of chopped tomatoes
1 teaspoon hot paprika (or 1 teaspoon
   sweet paprika and ½ teaspoon cayenne)
1 large cauliflower, grated
2 dozen cleaned mussels*
8 large unpeeled tiger prawns
Lemon wedges and chopped flat-leaf
   parsley to serve

PAELLA

You can add other meat or seafood to this – squid, monkfish, clams, rabbit, etc. Cook fish or seafood as briefly as possible.

1 Sprinkle the saffron over the chicken stock and put to one side. Pour a dash of olive oil into a large sauté pan and fry the chicken thighs until golden all over. Remove with a slotted spoon.

2 Add the onion and fry until starting to brown. Add the chorizo and garlic for the last couple of minutes. Return the chicken to the pan along with the tomatoes and paprika and simmer gently with the lid on until the chicken is tender, stirring now and then.

3 While the chicken is cooking, heat another dash of olive oil in a frying pan and add the grated cauliflower. Fry until starting to turn golden, then pour in the chicken stock. Keep stirring the cauliflower until it is tender and the stock has all but evaporated.

4 Turn up the heat under the chicken and bring to a brisk simmer. Drop in the mussels, clap on the lid and check after 2 minutes – they should all be open. If not, put the lid back on for another 30 seconds. Tip in the prawns and simmer for a minute, until the prawns are just cooked through and bright pink.

5 Stir the cauliflower 'rice' through the chicken and seafood mixture and put into a shallow serving dish. Serve with the parsley sprinkled over and lemon wedges on the side.

*Throw away any raw mussels that don't close when tapped with a knife. Throw away any cooked ones that don't open.

SERVES 2
Oil and butter for frying
2 large fillet steaks
½ teaspoon Marigold bouillon powder
75ml red wine

100ml double cream
50ml water
½ teaspoon mustard powder
75g Stilton cheese

FILLET STEAK IN A RED WINE AND STILTON SAUCE

1 Heat the oil and butter in a frying pan and fry the steaks to your liking. The easiest way to judge how well they are cooked is to press the middle of the steak with your finger and compare how that feels with either your cheek, the end of your nose or your chin. Rare should feel roughly as soft as your cheek, medium like the end of your nose and well done as firm as your chin.

2 Remove the steaks from the pan and keep warm. Drain off most of the fat and return the pan to the heat. Add the Marigold powder and stir around for a couple of seconds, then pour in the wine.

3 Bring to a simmer and allow to reduce to a syrupy consistency. Add the cream, water, mustard powder and Stilton and simmer again until the sauce thickens and the Stilton slumps into the sauce.

4 Serve the sauce with the steaks and some watercress or garlicky spinach.

SERVES 2
125g sliced almonds
1 onion, roughly chopped
2 fresh green chillies (less or more to taste)
5 cloves of garlic, peeled
125ml water
4 tablespoons groundnut oil
500g diced stewing beef or shoulder of lamb
5cm cinnamon stick

6 cloves
6 cardamom pods, pressed with your
   thumb to crack them open slightly
6 black peppercorns
1 tablespoon ground cumin
1 tablespoon ground coriander
250ml stock
284ml double cream
A few toasted almonds

BEEF KORMA

1 Preheat oven to 160°C, gas mark 3.

2 Put the almonds, onion, chillies and garlic into a blender with the water and blend to a paste.

3 Heat the oil in an ovenproof sauté pan or cast-iron casserole dish and fry the meat cubes until well browned on all sides.

4 Remove the meat with a slotted spoon and add the whole spices to the oil. Stir until they start to smell fragrant.

5 Add the paste from the blender to the pan and stir and fry until the paste has browned a little. Stir in the ground spices, then the browned meat.

6 Add the stock, cover tightly and put into the oven until the meat is meltingly tender. Check occasionally, and if it looks a bit dry add a little more stock or water.

7 Stir in the cream and return to the oven until heated through.

8 Serve sprinkled with toasted almonds. The whole spices aren't meant to be eaten.

SERVES 1
1 small fillet (100g) of hot-smoked
  salmon*
100g feta cheese, cubed
8 very small steamed broccoli florets

1 tablespoon chopped fresh parsley
  and dill, mixed
75g strong Cheddar cheese
2 large free-range eggs
140ml double cream

SALMON AND FETA BAKE

1 Preheat the oven to 190°C/gas mark 5.
Flake the salmon into a shallow ovenproof dish.
2 Sprinkle the feta, broccoli and herbs over and around the salmon and grate over 50g of the Cheddar.
3 Whisk together the eggs and cream and stir in. Grate over the rest of the cheese.
4 Bake for 25–30 minutes, until golden brown and puffed up.

*This would work with smoked mackerel too.

SERVES 4
1 small onion
1 clove of garlic, crushed
1 fat fresh red chilli
1 stick of lemongrass
Stalks from a bunch of fresh coriander
Juice of 1 lime

500g pork mince
1 rounded tablespoon peanut butter
1 heaped teaspoon unsweetened
   desiccated coconut
1 teaspoon fish sauce (nam pla)
2 teaspoons tamari soy sauce
groundnut oil for frying

THAI-STYLE MEATBALLS WITH PEANUT SAUCE

1 Put the peeled onion, garlic, chilli, lemongrass, coriander stalks and half the lime juice into a blender or a pestle and mortar and blitz to a paste. Add the paste to the pork mince and mix thoroughly. Leave in the fridge for a couple of hours.

2 To make the satay-style sauce, stir together the peanut butter, remaining lime juice, coconut, fish sauce and tamari. Add sufficient boiling water (about a tablespoon) to make a runny consistency. Leave to stand until the mince is ready to cook, then stir and add a little more water (it will thicken on standing).

3 Heat some groundnut oil in a frying pan. Take walnut-sized lumps of the mince, roll them into a ball, and flatten slightly – you are aiming for something that looks like a tiny beefburger. Fry briskly until golden brown on both sides.

4 Serve blisteringly hot, straight from the pan, on a bed of soft salad leaves drizzled with the peanut sauce.

SERVES 4
500g beef mince
150g ricotta cheese
1 egg
Salt and freshly ground black pepper
2 tablespoons finely chopped fresh parsley
Oil for frying

1 onion, finely sliced
250g button mushrooms
1 wineglass of white wine or dry cider
300ml beef stock
1 small carton of double cream, soured
    cream or crème fraîche
Extra chopped parsley for garnishing

MEATBALL STROGANOFF

1 Mix together the beef mince, ricotta, egg, salt and pepper and parsley. This is best done with your hands.

2 Wet your hands and form the meat mixture into small balls, approximately the same size as the mushrooms. Put in the fridge for an hour to firm up a little.

3 Heat the oil in a large frying pan and fry the onion gently until golden.

4 Remove the onion from the pan and add a little more oil. Add the mushrooms and fry quickly until just changing colour, then remove from the pan.

5 Add the meatballs a few at a time and fry briskly until they are well browned on all sides – this is important for the finished flavour of the dish. You may need to lower the heat slightly.

6 Return the onion, the mushrooms and all the meatballs to the pan, pour over the wine or cider and allow to bubble furiously for 1 minute. Add the stock, lower the heat, and simmer for 30 minutes. The stock should now be fairly well reduced. If not, simmer a little more briskly until you have about half the original amount of liquid.

7 Add the cream, stir gently to mix and allow to heat through for a couple of minutes.

8 Sprinkle with chopped parsley before serving.

9 Serve with leafy veg, butternut mash or cauliflower 'rice'.

▸ In Phase 3 serve with a small portion of brown Basmati rice.

SERVES 4
1 sliced onion
4 tablespoons groundnut oil
50g butter
8 cardamom pods, crushed
6 cloves
1 cinnamon stick

1 teaspoon each of the following: easy ginger, easy garlic, easy chilli, cumin seeds, coriander seeds, ground coriander, ground cumin
4 skinless, boneless chicken breasts
A 400g tin of chopped tomatoes
15g chopped fresh coriander
100ml double cream

BUTTER CHICKEN

1 Fry the onion in the oil and butter until deep golden brown.

2 Add the cardamom pods, cloves and cinnamon stick and stir around for a few seconds, then add the ginger, garlic, chilli, cumin seeds, coriander seeds, ground coriander and ground cumin.

3 Add the chicken, cut into chunks, then the chopped tomatoes.

4 Simmer gently for 10 minutes with the pan covered, then for 10 minutes with the lid off.

5 Add the chopped coriander and the cream and simmer gently for another 10 minutes, until the sauce is reduced and thickened and the oil is beginning to separate.

6 Serve with buttered spinach. The whole spices are not supposed to be eaten.

▸ In Phase 3 serve with a small portion of brown Basmati rice.

SERVES 4

1 large onion, diced
A 2.5cm piece of fresh ginger, peeled
2 large cloves of garlic
3 tablespoons olive oil
1 teaspoon cumin seeds
1–2 bay leaves
A 2.5cm piece of cinnamon stick
2 cardamom pods
5–6 black peppercorns

5–6 cloves
1/2 teaspoon turmeric powder
1/2 teaspoon chilli powder (more if you like it)
1 1/2 teaspoons ground coriander
A 400g tin of chopped tomatoes
500g mince (beef, lamb, pork or chicken)
Salt to taste
A small handful of chopped fresh coriander
1/2 teaspoon garam masala

KEEMA

1 Put the onion, ginger and garlic into a food processor
and pulse until finely chopped to a paste.

2 Heat the oil and add the cumin, bay leaves, cinnamon,
cardamoms, peppercorns and cloves. Fry for about a minute
until fragrant.

3 Add the paste from the food processor and fry until
lightly brown.

4 Add all the ground spices, except the garam masala, and
fry for a few seconds, then add the tomatoes and fry until the
oil separates.

5 Stir in the mince and fry until the meat is brown, then add
120ml of water and simmer over a low heat for approximately
20 minutes.

6 Taste and add salt if you think it needs it.

7 Serve sprinkled with fresh coriander and garam masala
(we like to drizzle a little cream over ours too).

▸ In Phase 3 serve with a small portion of brown Basmati rice.

SERVES 6–8

1 onion, sliced or diced
Oil for frying
2 cloves of garlic, smashed
2 fat fresh red chillies, finely chopped
500g minced beef
A 400g tin of chopped tomatoes
A squirt of tomato purée
120ml stock or water
1 tablespoon ground coriander
1 tablespoon ground cumin
1 tablespoon dried oregano
A handful of chopped fresh coriander

FOR THE TOPPING

4 large eggs, separated
80ml double cream
125g ricotta cheese
200g ground almonds
100g strong Cheddar cheese, grated
1 teaspoon baking powder
A large pinch of sea salt
Melted butter

BEE'S CHILLI BAKE

1 Preheat the oven to 180°C/gas mark 4.

Fry the onion in the oil until soft. Add the garlic and chillies, then the mince, and stir around, breaking up any lumps, until there are no red bits left in the mince.

2 Add the tomatoes, tomato purée, stock, ground spices and oregano. Stir well, bring to the boil, then cover and simmer over a very low heat for approximately 45 minutes. Remove the lid, turn up the heat and simmer briskly until most of the liquid has gone.

3 Stir in the fresh coriander. Put the meat mixture in the bottom of an ovenproof dish and leave to cool.

4 To make the topping, put the egg yolks, double cream and ricotta in a bowl and whisk until combined. In another bowl put the ground almonds, Cheddar, baking powder and salt. Mix together thoroughly.

5 In a scrupulously clean bowl and using scrupulously clean whisks, beat the egg whites until they form soft peaks. Mix the egg mixture into the ground almond mixture, then fold in the egg whites. Spoon the topping over the mince in the ovenproof dish. Brush the top with melted butter. Bake for approximately 30 minutes, until the topping has risen and is firm and golden brown.

6 Serve with buttered leafy green veg or salad.

SERVES 6, WITH LEFTOVERS
1 whole shoulder of lamb, skin lightly
   scored
1 large sprig of fresh rosemary

½ a head of garlic, unpeeled
A sprinkling of coarse salt
300ml red wine (use water or stock
   if you have no wine)

SLOW-ROAST SHOULDER OF LAMB

1 Preheat the oven to 120°C/gas mark 2.

2 Heat a large roasting tin on the top of the stove. Stick the shoulder of lamb in, skin side down, and brown it as well as you can.

3 Take the rosemary sprigs and 'wring' them as you would a dishcloth, to break up the cells in the leaves a little and release their oil. Lift up the lamb, put the rosemary into the tin, and sit the lamb on top, skin side up. Scatter the unpeeled garlic cloves (as many as you like) around the meat. Sprinkle over some coarse salt and add your liquid of choice to the pan. Cover with foil and put into the oven for a minimum of 4 hours. It will happily carry on for another 3 hours if need be.

4 This will not carve, though – you need to pull the meat off the bones with a couple of forks, easily done. In fact the bones will usually lift out without any problem. De-fat the juices (they're usually very fatty) and serve alongside if liked.

▸ Cold leftovers make a fab curry (see page 152)

1 onion
Oil for frying
½ a large butternut squash, peeled
    and cut into chunks
Seeds from 8 cardamom pods
3 cloves
1 stick of cinnamon
2 teaspoons coriander seeds
2 teaspoons cumin seeds
1 teaspoon crushed hot dried chillies

A 2.5cm piece of fresh ginger, peeled
    and grated
2 cloves of garlic
Cooked leftover lamb (amount not
    desperately important – even a very
    little would add depth and flavour)
A handful of fresh coriander
1 tin of coconut milk
8 nuggets of frozen spinach (or 1 large
    bag of fresh)

LAMB CURRY

1 Start by frying the onion in a little oil over a medium heat.
Add the squash and fry for about 5 minutes.

2 Add all the spices and flavourings and stir around for a minute
or two until fragrant.

3 Add the lamb, then the chopped coriander stalks and the
coconut milk. Add the spinach if using frozen (if using fresh,
add it at the end and stir until wilted).

4 Stir, cover and allow to putter gently until the squash
is cooked.

5 Sprinkle with the chopped coriander leaves and serve.

SERVES 6, WITH LEFTOVERS

A piece of belly pork, about 2kg
Coarse salt

A sprinkling of fennel seeds
A small quantity of crushed chillies

SLOW-ROAST BELLY PORK

1 Preheat the oven to 230°C/gas mark 8.

2 We buy the pork in one piece with the bones in and the skin on. If you don't have a seriously sharp knife at home, ask the butcher to score the skin as finely as possible.

3 Make sure the meat is dry. If you have had to resort to a supermarket, remove the meat from the plastic, put it on a plate and leave it overnight in the fridge to dry thoroughly.

4 Remove from the fridge half an hour before you want to cook it (this brings it up to room temperature).

5 Rub the scored skin with plenty of coarse salt, making sure you get some down into all the nooks and crannies. Sprinkle over the fennel seeds and crushed chillies.

6 Put the pork into a roasting tin, scored side up, and put the tin on a highish shelf in the oven. After 20 minutes turn the heat down to 160°C/gas 2 or 3 and move the meat to a middle shelf.

7 Cook for a minimum of 4 hours. It is ready when the meat is butter soft and falls off the bones.

SERVES 6–8

Olive oil for frying
1 small onion, sliced
6 best-quality pork sausages
8 boneless, skinless chicken thighs

225g chorizo sausage
1 tinned pimento (or 1 red pepper), sliced
1 tablespoon paprika
A 400g tin of chopped tomatoes
25g fresh flat-leaf parsley, chopped

SPANISH CHICKEN

1 Preheat the oven to 170°C/gas mark 3.
Heat the oil in a large ovenproof sauté pan or cast-iron casserole dish and fry the onion until golden. Add the sausages and brown on all sides, then do the same with the chicken thighs.

2 Chop the chorizo into bite-sized chunks and add to the pan along with the pimento or pepper, the paprika and the tin of tomatoes.

3 Put the lid on the pan and bung it all in the oven for about 2 hours or until the chicken is tender. Check halfway through, and if it looks a bit dry add a very little chicken stock or water.

4 Stir in the parsley before serving.

5 This would be lovely with any veggie mash, or cauli 'rice'.

▸ In Phase 3 add some whole new potatoes in their skins along with the tinned tomatoes.

SERVES 4

400g pork tenderloin	Oil and butter for frying
1 tub of ricotta cheese	3 leeks, cleaned and cut into 2cm pieces
165g tapenade	A knob of butter

PORK AND OLIVE RAVIOLI

1 Slice the tenderloin into 0.5cm slices. Place the slices between baking parchment and bat out gently, using the end of a rolling pin, until as thin as possible.

2 Mix together the ricotta and tapenade. Place ½ a teaspoon of the mixture on half the slices of pork and top with the rest to make 'ravioli', pressing the edges firmly.

3 Fry the 'ravioli' gently in oil and butter for approximately 7 minutes, until golden brown and cooked through.

4 Serve with buttered leeks: steam the leeks until tender, then add the butter and allow it to melt into the leeks.

▸ Tenderloin is easier to slice if it has been kept in the freezer for about 45 minutes.

olives

1 tin of coconut milk

125g button mushrooms

125g whole green beans

4 skinless, boneless chicken breasts, cut
into chunks

FOR THE PASTE

2 teaspoons coriander seeds

2 fresh green chillies (seeds removed if you prefer)

A 2cm piece of fresh ginger, peeled and roughly
chopped

2 shallots

2 cloves of garlic

Stalks from a handful of fresh coriander
(reserve the leaves)

A handful of fresh Thai basil (or ordinary basil
with some mint leaves added)

1 stalk of lemongrass, outer leaf removed,
bashed with a rolling pin and chopped

6 black peppercorns

Juice and zest of 2 limes

1 teaspoon fish sauce (nam pla)

1 teaspoon tamari soy sauce

THAI GREEN CHICKEN CURRY

1 Put the coriander seeds into a small frying pan and dry-fry for a couple of minutes, until the seeds smell fragrant and are sizzling very slightly. Remove the pan from the heat and use a pestle and mortar to crush them.

2 Put the crushed seeds with all the other paste ingredients into a blender and whiz to a paste with a tablespoon of water. Stop the blender now and then and scrape down the sides.

3 Put the coconut milk into a wok and bring to the boil. Reduce the heat and simmer gently for about 10 minutes until it has reduced by about a third.

4 Stir in the paste, add the vegetables and the chicken and simmer for another 5 minutes, or until the chicken is cooked.

5 Remove from the heat and let the curry stand for 5 minutes before serving, to allow the sauce to thicken slightly.

▸ In Phase 3 serve with a small portion of brown Basmati rice.

SERVES 4

6 good-quality thick pork sausages
Oil for frying
1 bag of spinach
100ml stock, made with Marigold
   bouillon powder

250g mascarpone cheese
1 small butternut squash, cooked
   and mashed

SAUSAGE CASSEROLE

1 Preheat the oven to 180°C/gas mark 4.

2 Brown the sausages under a grill, or in a little oil in a pan. Cut into chunks and arrange in the bottom of an ovenproof casserole dish.

3 Put the spinach into a colander. Boil the kettle and pour the water over the spinach until wilted (sometimes you need to do this twice to wilt it). Put a saucer over the spinach in the colander and press down to squeeze out as much water as possible.

4 Tip the spinach on to a chopping board and chop with a sharp knife. Sprinkle it over the sausages.

5 Whisk the stock into the mascarpone and pour over the spinach and sausages.

6 Cover with the butternut squash mash and brush with a little melted butter.

7 Put the dish into the oven and bake until the top is golden.

▸ In Phase 3, add some cooked Puy lentils along with the spinach.

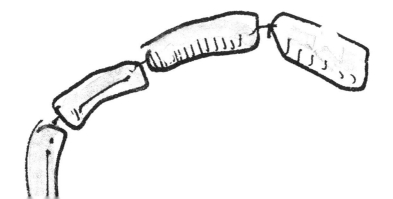

6 Toulouse sausages
A splash of olive oil
2 leeks, cleaned and sliced

A 400g tin of chopped tomatoes
A squirt of tomato purée
1 teaspoon cider vinegar
A handful of grated Parmesan cheese

ANOTHER SAUSAGE CASSEROLE

1 Preheat the oven to 180°C/gas mark 4.

2 Skin the sausages and split each one into three. Roll each piece to make a ball. Heat the oil in a shallow pan and fry the sausage balls until brown all over.

3 Remove the sausage balls from the pan with a slotted spoon and place in an ovenproof casserole dish.

4 Add the leeks to the pan. Stir and fry for a couple of minutes, then tip in the chopped tomatoes, tomato purée and cider vinegar.

5 Bring to the boil, then turn down the heat and simmer gently for 5 minutes.

6 Pour the mixture over the sausage balls, cover the casserole with a lid or foil and put into the oven for 30 minutes.

Sprinkle with Parmesan cheese and serve with buttered cabbage.

SERVES 3

2 large leeks, trimmed, cleaned and finely sliced	230g cooked ham, diced
Butter and oil for frying	230g crumbled Stilton cheese
120ml white wine	1 whole celeriac, mashed
120ml double cream	30g flaked almonds
	Melted butter for brushing

HAM, LEEK AND BLUE CHEESE PIE

1 Preheat the oven to 180°C/gas mark 4.

2 Fry the leeks in the oil and butter until softened and turning golden.

3 Pour over the white wine and allow to bubble until reduced to a syrupy consistency.

4 Add the cream, ham and Stilton and turn off the heat. Allow the cheese to slump into the sauce.

5 Put the mixture into a lasagne-type oven dish. Top with the celeriac mash, sprinkle with the flaked almonds and brush with melted butter.

6 Bake in the oven until golden.

7 Absolutely lovely with some buttered Savoy cabbage.

1 cauliflower, separated into florets

1 green pepper, seeds removed, diced

1 medium onion, halved and thickly sliced

2 tablespoons olive oil

A 340g tin of corned beef, diced

A handful of fresh parsley, chopped

CORNED BEEF HASH

1 Preheat the oven to 220°C/gas mark 7.

Put the cauliflower florets, diced pepper and onion slices into a mixing bowl.

2 Pour over the oil and mix around until everything is evenly coated.

3 Spread out in a shallow roasting dish and put into the oven for 20 minutes, or until everything is tender and tinged here and there with brown.

4 Scatter over the diced corned beef and put back into the oven for 5 minutes to heat through.

5 Stir in the chopped parsley and serve.

SERVES 4

1 large aubergine
Olive oil
200g feta cheese
5 nuggets of frozen spinach

2 eggs, beaten
2 tablespoons double cream
Salt and freshly ground black pepper
A little grated nutmeg

AUBERGINE, SPINACH AND FETA PIE

1 Preheat the oven to 180°C/gas mark 4.
Slice the aubergine thinly lengthwise. Brush with a little olive oil and grill, fry or griddle until softened but not mushy.

2 Crumble the feta into a bowl and mash with a fork, but don't mash it to a paste – you want it to have some texture.

3 Microwave the spinach nuggets for approximately 4 minutes, or until heated through. Tip into a sieve and run under the cold tap, then, using your hands, squeeze out as much water as possible. Use some kitchen scissors to chop the spinach straight into the feta cheese. Stir in the beaten eggs and double cream and season with salt, pepper and nutmeg.

4 Lay the aubergine slices in an ovenproof pie dish like petals, with the fat end of the slice in the middle of the dish and the thin end hanging over the side – there will be gaps between the slices, but don't worry about that.

5 Spread the cheese mixture over the aubergines, then fold over the ends of the slices to cover – again there will be gaps.

6 Bake in the centre of the oven for 30–35 minutes, or until the pie is golden brown and just firm to the touch.

SERVES 1
A small handful of black peppercorns
A knob of butter
1 beef steak, weighing about 100–150g

A glug of double cream
Torn lettuce leaves
½ an avocado, sliced
Blue cheese dressing (see recipe on page 210)

STEAK AU POIVRE

1 Crush the peppercorns in a pestle and mortar or a clean coffee grinder. Melt a knob of butter in a pan. Press the peppercorns into both sides of the steak so that they stick. When the butter sizzles, add the steak and turn up the heat to medium.

2 Flip the steak over after a couple of minutes. It should be nice and crusty on one side. To test, poke the middle of the steak firmly with a finger. Springy, rare; less springy, medium; firm, well done.

3 Remove the steak to a plate. Pour the cream into the buttery/steaky juices, let it bubble for a couple of seconds, then pour over the steak.

4 Serve with lettuce and avocado (and blue cheese dressing if you wish).

SERVES 1

1 organic chicken breast	A bunch of fresh tarragon, chopped
A knob of butter	1 small tub of double cream
A glug of groundnut oil	Juice of ½ a lemon

TARRAGON CHICKEN

1 Cut the chicken into strips, or chunks if you prefer. Melt the butter in the pan on a medium heat and add a tiny glug of groundnut oil. When the butter is sizzling, add the tarragon and the chicken strips, and cook until the strips go crispy and brown (if crispy and brown and a bit sticky is what you like).

2 Add enough cream to make a sauce – a third to half of the small tub should do it. Wait a minute for it all to meld and bubble.

3 Add the lemon juice, taste, and season if you think it needs it.

4 Serve with cauliflower faux-mash (see page 214).

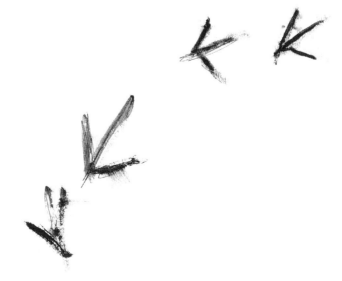

1 cod fillet
Good-quality olive oil
½ a tomato, sliced

A generous handful of any fresh herb, or
mixture of fresh herbs (try thyme and
rosemary)

ROAST COD WITH HERBS
AND TOMATOES

1 Preheat the oven to 190°C/gas mark 5.
Brush the cod fillet – and it doesn't have to be cod, it could be
any other robust and fresh-looking fish – with olive oil. Cover
with sliced tomato.

2 Crush the herbs a little so they release their fragrance, and lay
them on top of the cod.

3 Wrap the whole thing up neatly in foil and roast for 15 minutes.

4 Serve with a salad – it's nice with rocket and Parmesan. Don't
forget to pour the herby olive oil that's puddled at the bottom
of the foil on to the fish when you serve it.

SERVES 4–6

FOR THE FILLING
1.5kg extra lean minced beef
2 medium onions, finely sliced
2 sticks of celery, finely chopped
1 teaspoon fresh thyme leaves
1 tablespoon tomato purée
Salt and freshly ground black pepper
230g mushrooms, chopped

2 tablespoons butter
FOR THE TOPPING
900g trimmed cauliflower
60ml soured cream
230g grated Cheddar cheese
2 tablespoons butter
1 egg
8 rashers of bacon, cooked and crumbled

FAKE SHEPHERD'S PIE

1 Preheat the oven to 180°C/gas mark 4.
Put the beef into a large pan and cook over high heat until it stops looking red and raw. Add the onions, celery, thyme, tomato purée, salt and pepper.

2 Cover the pan, turn the heat right down and cook for 30 minutes, stirring from time to time. Add some water if it looks too dry.

3 Fry the mushrooms in the butter and add to the beef. Cook for 15 minutes more.

4 Meanwhile, make the topping: steam the cauliflower until almost mushy, about 15 minutes. Blend in a food processor, adding the soured cream, cheese and butter. Add the egg and whiz again. Mix in the bacon.

5 Assemble the shepherd's pie and bake in the oven for 45–50 minutes.

MAKES 4 FISHCAKES
1 fresh red chilli, sliced
4 spring onions
A handful of fresh coriander, chopped
1 egg

2 teaspoons finely chopped lemongrass
(the 'lazy' lemongrass in jars is fine)
200g salmon
Salt and freshly ground black pepper
Olive oil

THAI SALMON FISHCAKES

1 Put the chilli, spring onions, coriander, egg and lemongrass into a blender and whiz to a paste. Add the salmon and salt and pepper to taste and blend again until the texture is similar to mince. It will be quite sloppy, but don't panic.

2 Heat a good puddle of oil in a frying pan.

3 Blob tablespoons of the mixture into the pan. If it starts to spit, turn the heat down. Let one side really seal properly before trying to turn over (like an omelette). When the fishcakes are firm and golden brown, they are ready.

4 Delicious served with a squeeze of lime juice and black pepper and some stir-fried cabbage.

SERVES 4
2 large onions
3 courgettes
4–5 field mushrooms
200g broccoli
200g cauliflower

1–2 cloves of garlic, sliced (or in chunks
    if you feel brave)
2 tablespoons olive oil
1kg lean braising steak
A pinch or two of dried chilli
Beef or vegetable stock, approx. 600ml
    (depends on size of your cooking pot)

COMFORTING BEEF STEW

1 Chop all the vegetables into big chunks and set aside.

2 Heat the oil in a large saucepan and brown the meat. Keep frying to seal it on all sides until golden brown. Remove the meat from the pan to a plate and set aside.

3 Fry the onions and garlic in the pan with the meat juices, allowing them to colour slightly. Return the meat to the pan, adding enough stock to cover.

4 Bring to a light boil and stir to loosen all the flavours from the bottom. Leave to simmer gently for 1 hour with the lid off, until the meat is tender.

5 Add the vegetables. You can use any of the vegetables from the 'allowed' list for this – but remember to put the harder vegetables in first, and the softer ones last, otherwise they'll turn to mush. Put the lid on and simmer for a further 15–20 minutes.

6 Serve with cauliflower faux-mash (see page 214) and a salad.

2 French-trimmed racks of lamb
3 cloves of garlic, crushed
2 teaspoons grated ginger
2 teaspoons white wine vinegar
A handful of finely chopped fresh
   mint leaves

2 teaspoons ground cumin
2 teaspoons ground coriander
1 teaspoon chilli powder
Sea salt
150ml yoghurt

MARINATED SPICED LAMB

1 Preheat the oven to 200°C/gas mark 6.
Put the lamb into a shallow dish.

2 Blend together the garlic, ginger, vinegar, mint, cumin, coriander, chilli, salt and yoghurt in a food processor. Pour this mixture over the lamb, cover, and refrigerate for at least 3 hours (overnight is best).

3 About half an hour before you want to eat, lay the lamb on a lined baking sheet and cook for 20 minutes if you like it pink, longer if you don't.

4 Remove from the oven and allow it to rest for 10 minutes before cutting into cutlets.

SERVES 4

100g Gorgonzola or other blue
cheese, crumbled
4 tablespoons soured cream
1 tablespoon mayonnaise

1 tablespoon red wine vinegar
1 teaspoon minced garlic
Salt and freshly ground black pepper
4 Portobello mushrooms
Extra virgin olive oil

GRILLED PORTOBELLO MUSHROOMS WITH BLUE CHEESE DRESSING

1 Mash the cheese to a paste. Stir in the soured cream, mayonnaise, vinegar and garlic. Season to taste and set aside.

2 Remove the stem from each mushroom and scrape out the gills with a small spoon. Score the tops in a cross-hatch pattern. Sprinkle the mushrooms with olive oil, and season with salt and pepper.

3 Grill for 2–3 minutes on each side until cooked through. Drizzle the cheese dressing on top.

4 Serve with a green salad.

Olive oil

400g beef fillet (250g if using as
   a starter for 2 people)

Sea salt and freshly ground black pepper

A fist-sized piece of Parmesan cheese

2 bags of rocket

TAGLIATA WITH ROCKET AND PARMESAN

1 Glug a couple of spoonfuls of olive oil into a cast-iron frying pan. Get it very hot, then chuck in the beef fillet and sear on all sides, over a high heat, turning frequently for about 15 minutes (you're aiming for a crusty, slightly blackened outside and a rare inside).

2 Take off the heat and leave the beef to sit for 10 minutes, then carve in thin slices (an electric knife works best).

3 Using a potato peeler, make thin shavings of Parmesan and arrange these on top of the beef.

4 Serve the beef on a bed of rocket, dressed, if you like, with salt, pepper and olive oil.

SERVES 4
4 rashers of smoked streaky bacon,
    chopped
Grated zest of 1 lemon

15g fresh flat-leaf parsley, chopped
15g fresh thyme, chopped
25g softened butter
1 free-range oven-ready chicken

TWO WAYS WITH A ROAST CHICKEN

ROASTING A CHICKEN TO EAT ON ITS OWN OR WITH SALAD

1 Preheat the oven to 180°C/gas mark 4.

2 Put the bacon, lemon zest and herbs into a food processor and pulse to a thick paste. Use a fork to blend the paste into the butter.

3 Carefully slide your fingers under the breast skin of the chicken, releasing it from the breast meat and forming a pocket on either side of the breastbone. Put a tablespoon of the paste into the cavity of the chicken and push half of the remaining mixture into each pocket, securing the skin with a cocktail stick if necessary.

4 Roast the chicken for about 1 hour, until the juices run clear from the thickest part of the thigh when poked with a skewer.

SERVES 4
1 lemon
1 free-range oven-ready chicken
Salt and freshly ground black pepper

A knob of butter
25g fresh tarragon
2 egg yolks
120ml double cream

CHICKEN WITH AN EGG AND LEMON SAUCE

1 Preheat the oven to 180°C/gas mark 4.

2 Cut the lemon in half and squeeze it over the skin of the chicken. Season the skin with salt and pepper, then put the squeezed lemon halves into the cavity of the chicken along with the butter and tarragon.

3 Roast the bird for about 1 hour, until the juices run clear from the thickest part of the thigh when poked with a skewer.

4 Take the chicken out of the roasting tin and drain off most of the fat, leaving behind all the juices and any sticky bits. Place the tin over a low heat on the hob. Whisk together the egg yolks, double cream and a splash of cold water, then whisk this mixture into the chicken juices. Continue to whisk vigorously until thickened, but do not boil. Serve with the chicken.

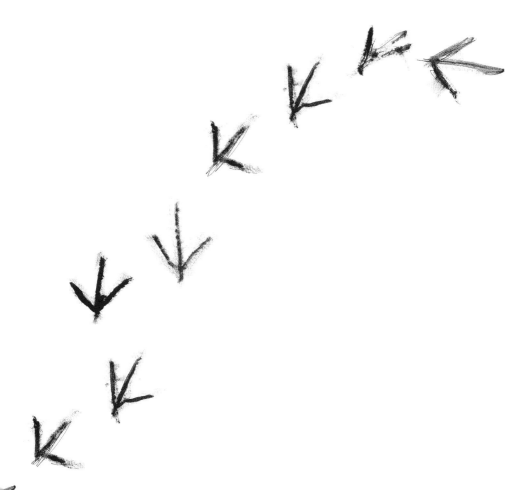

CHAPTER TWELVE

EASY WAYS WITH ...

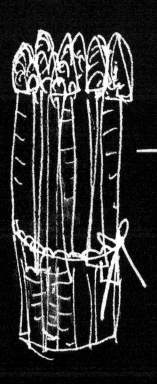

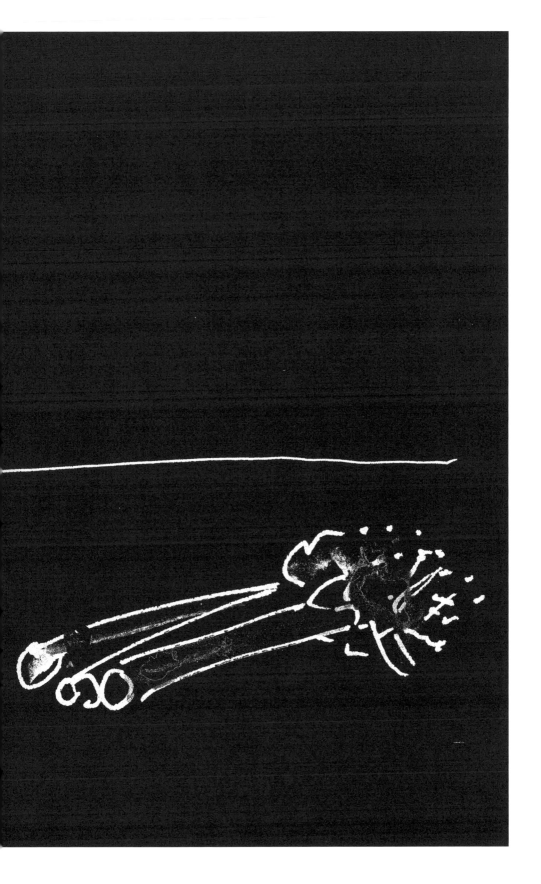

For when you're bored with vegetables and are staring into your fridge in an uninspired, possibly mutinous manner. These work as side dishes, as snacky things to pick at, or as main courses.

Asparagus

Rub the asparagus with olive oil. Griddle until tender. Scatter with Parmesan shavings.

Or steam until tender and serve with melted butter, or serve at room temperature with mayonnaise mixed with lemon juice and zest.

Brussels sprouts

Trim the outer leaves from the sprouts and slice the insides finely. Stir-fry with sliced garlic and ginger until bright green and just tender. Add a splash of dry sherry and allow to bubble away before serving.

Or trim the sprouts and steam until tender. Chop finely in the pan with a sharp knife. Add cream and crumbled blue cheese and allow to stand until the cheese has melted.

Cabbage

Shred finely and stir-fry in a little oil. Add sesame oil and tamari soy sauce to taste.

Or crispy bacon bits and grainy mustard.

Celery

Put washed celery stalks into a shallow baking dish. Add enough stock to come halfway up the stalks. Cover the dish tightly with foil and bake in a medium oven (180°C/gas mark 4) until soft when prodded with a fork. Drain the juices into a bowl, mix with a tub of mascarpone and some grated Parmesan cheese, and spoon this mixture over the braised celery. Grill until browned in places and bubbling.

Or chop the braised celery into chunks and mix the chunks and juices with some tomato purée and a little curry powder. Top with grated cheese mixed with a little desiccated coconut, and grill until brown.

Courgettes

Use a swivel peeler along the length of the courgettes to make slender ribbons. Steam briefly until tender and dress with a little oil and lemon juice.

Or cut the courgettes into 1cm rounds and fry briskly in oil and butter with garlic and fresh rosemary.

French beans

Top and tail the beans and steam until tender. Stir in double cream and English mustard.

Or steam the beans until tender, then fry sliced cloves of garlic in oil and butter until just turning golden. Pour the hot garlic, oil and butter over the beans and serve immediately.

Kale

Wash 1kg of curly kale, cut out any tough stems, then stack the leaves and cut into 2cm slices. Fry 2 crushed cloves of garlic in a little olive oil and butter until barely golden, and add the kale and 100ml of stock. Cover the pan tightly and braise gently for 15 minutes.

Kale makes great Chinese 'seaweed'. Wash and dry the kale thoroughly, remove any tough stems, stack the leaves and cut into very fine ribbons – about 2–3mm thick. Heat 2cm of groundnut oil in a deep frying pan or wok and fry small handfuls of kale for 20–30 seconds. Remove with a slotted spoon and drain on crumpled kitchen paper. Mix together a teaspoon each of salt and Splenda and use to season the 'seaweed'.

Leeks

Cut the cleaned leeks into 6cm logs. Steam until tender. Wrap each log in a slice of good ham. Cover with mascarpone cheese sauce (see page 212) and grill until golden and bubbling.

Or slice the leeks finely and stir-fry briskly in groundnut oil with garlic, ginger and sesame seeds. Sprinkle with tamari soy sauce before serving.

Mangetout peas

Steam the mangetout until tender, then stir through a large knob of butter and lots of freshly grated Parmesan cheese.

Or stir-fry the mangetout with chopped spring onions in a little groundnut oil until tender. Stir in a large handful of finely chopped fresh mint and a knob of butter.

Pak choy

Cut the pak choy in half lengthways. Place in a wok with a crushed clove of garlic, 1 cm of fresh ginger, peeled and grated, and 2 tablespoons each of tamari soy sauce, rice wine vinegar and sesame oil. Bring to a simmer, cover the wok with a lid or foil, and cook until the pak choy is tender.

Or steam baby pak choy until tender and drizzle with chilli oil and freshly squeezed lime juice.

Spinach

Rinse well, pack into a Pyrex dish, cover with clingfilm and microwave until collapsed. Drain very well in a sieve, pressing down with a saucer or small plate. Stir in butter and horseradish.

Or a little cream and freshly grated nutmeg.

CHAPTER THIRTEEN
CANAPÉS

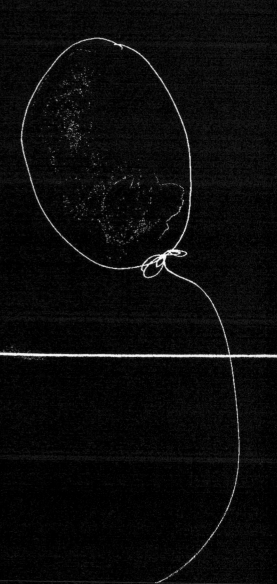

For parties. Because being on a diet doesn't mean you can't 'entertain', as Abigail and her kaftan would say. You can! You must! But don't drink wine, or punch, or any other sugar-laden stuff. Drink spirits.

SMOKED SALMON BLINIS

MAKES ABOUT 24
1 large egg
30ml double cream
60ml ground almonds
A large pinch of baking powder
Oil for frying
1 small packet of smoked salmon trimmings
125ml cream, whipped

1 Whisk together the egg, cream, almonds and baking powder to make a smooth batter.

2 Heat some oil in a non-stick frying pan. Use a teaspoon to dollop batter into the pan to make tiny pancakes. Fry until golden on both sides.

3 Top each pancake with a small piece of smoked salmon and a little whipped cream.

SALAMI AND CREAM CHEESE CORNETS

MAKES 12
12 slices of salami
A 200g tub of cream cheese

1 Cut each slice of salami in half. Take one half and roll the corners together, then slide one corner under the other to make a cornet. Press the edges together firmly.

2 Whisk some cream cheese until softened and smooth.

3 Pipe or spoon the cheese into the cornets – if they refuse to stay rolled, spike with a cocktail stick.

STUFFED EGGS

MAKES 24
12 quail's eggs, hard-boiled, shelled and halved
2 teaspoons mayonnaise
A pinch of Cajun seasoning
A small jar of fish roe

1 Put the cooked egg yolks into a small bowl and mash them with a little mayonnaise and a pinch of Cajun seasoning.

2 Spoon or pipe the mixture back into the egg white halves and top each one with a tiny amount of fish roe (you won't need the whole jar).

AUBERGINE WRAPS

MAKES 24

2 long slender aubergines, cut into 24 rounds
200g feta cheese, cut into 24 cubes
24 small fresh mint leaves
Oil for frying

1 Fry the aubergine slices until golden on both sides and soft.

2 Wrap each slice around a cube of feta cheese and a mint leaf and secure with a cocktail stick.

KILTED SAUSAGES

MAKES 24

4 chipolata sausages
12 rashers of streaky bacon, cut in half

1 Wrap each sausage in a piece of bacon.

2 Lay them in a small roasting tin and bake at 180°C/gas 4, turning occasionally, until the bacon is brown and crisp and the sausages are cooked.

CHEESE AND ONION BITES

MAKES ABOUT 24

1 recipe quantity of Parmesan Crisps (see page 94), made very tiny
Oil and butter
1 small onion, halved and finely sliced
A dash of double cream
A few fresh thyme leaves

1 Make the tiny Parmesan crisps and leave to cool.

2 Heat a little oil and butter in a small frying pan and fry the onion long and slow, until deep golden brown.

3 Turn up the heat, add a dash of cream and bubble until thickened.

4 Stir in the thyme leaves and allow to cool.

5 Top each Parmesan crisp with a little of the onion mixture and serve immediately.

STUFFED TOMATOES

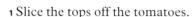

MAKES 24
24 cherry tomatoes
1 packet of Boursin cheese (garlic and herb or black pepper)
1 tablespoon double cream
2 tablespoons finely chopped fresh parsley

1 Slice the tops off the tomatoes.

2 Use a small spoon to remove the seeds and pulp from each tomato and discard.

3 Mash the Boursin with a little double cream to soften, and spoon into each tomato.

4 Sprinkle with a little parsley.

SPICY KING PRAWNS WITH TAMARIND DIP

MAKES 24
24 cooked king prawns
Tabasco sauce
Juice of ½ a lime
3 tablespoons tamarind pulp
1 tablespoon cider vinegar
Chopped fresh coriander
A pinch of ground cumin
A pinch of ground coriander
A pinch of Splenda

1 Put the prawns into a bowl and pour on the lime juice and approximately 8 dashes of Tabasco sauce. Leave to marinate for an hour or so.

2 To make the dip, mix together the rest of the ingredients.

3 Serve the dip in a ramekin or small bowl, with the prawns and cocktail sticks.

KOFTE

MAKES ABOUT 24
½ teaspoon cumin seeds
1 small onion, finely chopped
A little oil
30g ground almonds
1 fresh red or green chilli, finely chopped
A pinch of ground coriander
A pinch of ground cumin
250g lean minced lamb
1 small egg
20g toasted pine nuts, roughly chopped
1 tablespoon chopped fresh mint
1 tablespoon chopped fresh coriander
100ml double cream
3 tablespoons finely chopped fresh mint

1 Fry the cumin seeds and onion in a little oil until softened. Allow to cool.

2 Put into a food processor with all the other ingredients except the cream and the 3 tablespoons of mint and blitz to a paste.

3 With wet hands shape 1 teaspoon of the mixture into a tiny meatball. Repeat with the rest of the mixture.

4 Fry the meatballs for approximately 6 minutes in a little oil until browned all over and cooked through. Drain on kitchen paper.

5 Mix together the cream and remaining mint to make a dip. Use cocktail sticks to serve the warm kofte with the creamy mint dip.

EGG AND BACON NESTS

MAKES 24
8 slices of Parma ham
2 hard-boiled eggs, mashed with mayonnaise

1 Preheat the oven to 200°C/gas 6.

2 Cut each slice of ham into three and use to line two 12-hole mini bun tins, scrunching the ham to fit if necessary.

3 Bake for 5 minutes, or until crisp and brown. Allow to cool, then remove from the tins.

4 Use a small spoon to fill the ham cases with the egg mayonnaise. Serve immediately.

CHICKEN SATAY

MAKES 24
3 large skinless, boneless chicken breasts
1 teaspoon ground cumin
1 teaspoon ground coriander
1/2 teaspoon turmeric
1 teaspoon easy garlic
1 teaspoon Splenda
1 tablespoon tamari soy sauce
1 tablespoon lemon juice
1 teaspoon fish sauce (nam pla)
A little oil
PEANUT DIPPING SAUCE
100g crunchy peanut butter
Juice of 1 lime
1 tablespoon fish sauce (nam pla)
1 teaspoon Splenda
2 tablespoons of desiccated coconut
A pinch of chilli powder

1 Put the chicken in the freezer for 30 minutes – this will make it easier to slice thinly. Slice each chicken breast lengthways into 8.
2 Mix together the rest of the ingredients in a bowl and add the chicken. Leave overnight in the fridge to marinate.
3 When you're ready to cook, take each slice of chicken and 'zig-zag' it on to a bamboo skewer. Brush with oil and grill for 2 minutes each side until golden brown and crispy.
4 To make the dipping sauce, mix all the ingredients together in a bowl and add enough hot water to make a dipping consistency.

CRAB MAYONNAISE

MAKES ABOUT 24
250g fresh crabmeat
2 tablespoons mayonnaise
Finely grated zest of 1 lemon

1 Mix the crabmeat with the mayonnaise and lemon zest.
2 Tear some Little Gem lettuce leaves in half or thirds, and spoon the crabmeat mixture on to the lettuce.

SEARED TUNA CARPACCIO WITH SESAME AND LIME

MAKES 18–24
Oil for frying
100g tuna steak, trimmed to a neat oblong
Juice of 1 lime
1 teaspoon sesame seeds

1 Heat a teaspoon of oil in a small non-stick frying pan and sear the tuna for 30 seconds on each side. Remove from the pan.
2 Add the sesame seeds to the pan and stir-fry until golden brown.
3 Using a very sharp knife, slice the tuna as thinly as possible and lay the slices out on a plate. Drizzle with lime juice and sprinkle with the toasted sesame seeds, then fold or twist on to cocktail sticks.

MINIATURE SCONES WITH STRAWBERRIES AND CREAM

MAKES ABOUT 24
Basic almond sponge (see page 215)
Fresh strawberries
Whipped double cream

1 Using a 2cm cutter, stamp out as many 'scones' as possible from the almond sponge.
2 Pipe or spoon a swirl of whipped cream on to the top of each scone and garnish each one with half a strawberry.

CHOCOLATE CUPS WITH CINNAMON MASCARPONE MOUSSE

MAKES ABOUT 22
1 egg white
1 tub of mascarpone cheese
A pinch of cinnamon (or to taste)
1 tube of M&S Dark Swiss Chocolates, unwrapped
A little finely grated dark chocolate or cocoa powder

1 Whisk the egg white to the stiff peak stage. Beat the mascarpone until smooth. Fold the egg white and cinnamon into the mascarpone.
2 Spoon or pipe the mixture on to the chocolate coins and dust with grated chocolate or cocoa powder.

THAI BEEF SALAD

MAKES 24
Use the Thai beef salad recipe on page 120.

Cut 12 Little Gem leaves in half and spoon the salad on to
the lettuce.

PÂTÉ BITES

MAKES 24

Take 24 slices from a slender cucumber. Spoon a little chicken
liver pâté (see page 81) on to each slice and top with a quartered
slice of gherkin.

CRAB CAKES

MAKES ABOUT 24

Using half the quantity of the recipe on page 76, make tiny
crab cakes.

BHAJIAS

MAKES ABOUT 24

Using half the quantity of the recipes on pages 78 and 79, make
tiny bhajias.

CHAPTER FOURTEEN

DESSERTS

OK, truth time: I (India) don't eat puddings. Not ever, unless you include strawberries, raspberries and cheese. But if you must (and only from Phase 2 onwards please, eating these in Phase 1 will completely derail you), then have these. Have them in moderation, every now and then, and not every day.

SERVES 10–12

100g hazelnuts
150g ground almonds
A pinch of salt
125g butter
300g Philadelphia cheese

250g mascarpone cheese
250g ricotta cheese
150ml double cream
150ml soured cream
6 eggs, separated
Zest of 1 large unwaxed lemon

BAKED CHEESECAKE

1 Preheat the oven to 170°C/gas mark 3.

2 Put the hazelnuts into a dry frying pan and heat gently until they go a slightly darker brown. Put them straight into a food processor and whiz to the size of digestive biscuit crumbs. Pour the crumbs into a bowl and add the ground almonds and salt.

3 Melt the butter, pour it over the nuts and mix thoroughly to combine. Tip into a 24cm springform tin, base-lined with baking parchment, and spread out gently with the back of a spoon to get it evenly covered. Once spread out, press firmly with the back of the spoon to pack the mixture down as evenly as possible. Put into the fridge for about half an hour to set.

4 Put all the cheeses into a large mixing bowl and whisk until smooth. Add the creams, the egg yolks, a pinch of salt and the lemon zest and beat again until smooth and creamy.

5 Wash and dry the beaters thoroughly (any mixture left on them will stop the whites from whisking properly) and put the egg whites into a large mixing bowl. Whisk until they form stiff peaks – you should be able to tip the bowl upside down over your head without it falling out …

6 Take a large metal spoon and stir a third of the egg white into the cheese mixture to loosen it. Gently fold in the other two-thirds until no streaks of egg white can be seen. Pour the topping into the tin and level it with the back of a spoon.

7 Bake for 1¼–1½ hours, until the top is bronzed and the cheesecake feels slightly wobbly but not floppy when lightly pressed. Turn off the oven and leave to cool for one hour (it will sink quite a bit).

8 Open the door and leave for another hour, then chill thoroughly overnight in the fridge. DO NOT under any circumstances attempt to remove the tin too early, otherwise the edge will fall off on to the floor.

SERVES 2–4
1 sachet of sugar-free raspberry jelly
    (or any other flavour you want)

120ml boiling water
120ml cold water
230ml double cream

RASPBERRY MOUSSE

1 Put the jelly crystals into a large mixing bowl and pour over the boiling water. Immediately start whisking to dissolve the jelly.

2 When it looks like most of the crystals have gone, add the cold water and continue whisking. It will froth up a bit.

3 Add the double cream and continue to whisk until the mixture is cold and quite stiff.

4 Put into the fridge for about 30 minutes, until set.

5 You could decorate the mousse with whipped cream rosettes and chopped nuts/hundreds and thousands/gold and silver dragees/rose petals or SpongeBob Squarepants jelly sweets - whatever floats your particular boat. Or just eat it plain with a large spoon like we do …

100g hazelnuts
150g ground almonds
125g butter
2 sachets of lemon and lime sugar-free jelly

250g mascarpone cheese*
250g ricotta cheese*
230ml carton of double cream

LEMON AND LIME CHEESECAKE

1 Base-line a 24cm springform tin with baking parchment. Put the hazelnuts into a dry frying pan and heat gently until they go a slightly darker brown. You might hear a faint sizzling. Put them straight into a food processor and whiz to the size of digestive biscuit crumbs. Pour them into a bowl and add the ground almonds and a pinch of salt.

2 Melt the butter, pour over the nuts and mix thoroughly to combine. Tip into the base-lined tin and spread out gently with the back of a spoon, trying to get it evenly covered. Once spread out, press firmly with the back of the spoon to pack the mixture down as evenly as possible. Put into the fridge for about half an hour to set.

3 Put the jelly crystals into a bowl and pour over approximately 150ml of boiling water. Whisk vigorously until the crystals have dissolved. Allow to cool until tepid, whisking occasionally.

4 Put the cheese and cream into a mixing bowl and whisk together until all the lumps have gone and the mixture is smooth and creamy. Beat in the jelly a little at a time. Pour the mixture on to the cooled cheesecake base and refrigerate until set.

* 600g of Philadelphia cheese would work just as well in place of the mascarpone and ricotta.

SERVES 3

3 large handfuls of medium oatmeal	Splenda to taste (optional)
450ml double cream	1 punnet of raspberries
A dash of whisky	Fresh mint leaves for garnish

CRANACHAN

1 Put the oats into a frying pan over a low heat and stir with a wooden spoon until toasted and fragrant.

2 Whip the cream, but not too stiffly, only to the soft and floppy stage. Fold in the whisky, Splenda (if using), toasted oatmeal and most of the raspberries.

3 Pile into dessert glasses and garnish with mint leaves and the reserved raspberries.

SERVES 4
2 large eggs, separated
60ml double cream
2 tablespoons Splenda (optional)

A pinch of salt
Grated zest and juice of 1 large lemon
120g ground almonds
1 teaspoon baking powder

LEMON SPONGE PUDDING

You can flavour this with whatever takes your fancy – cocoa, orange, apple – depending on which phase you are doing.

1 Preheat the oven to 170°C/gas mark 3.

2 In a large Pyrex bowl, mix the egg yolks, cream, Splenda (if using), salt and lemon zest until smooth. Whisk in the ground almonds and baking powder until smooth.

3 Place the egg whites in a separate bowl and beat with an electric mixer or a hand whisk until soft peaks form.

4 Quickly stir the lemon juice into the almond mixture, followed by a large spoonful of the beaten egg whites, then fold in the remaining whites.

5 Bake for 30–40 minutes, until just springy to the touch. Serve with cream or real custard.

SERVES 4–6

650ml double cream
4 egg yolks
2 tablespoons Splenda

1 recipe quantity of lemon sponge
    pudding (see page 198)
1 punnet of raspberries

TRIFLE

1 Place 200ml of the double cream in a saucepan. Heat over a low to medium heat until the cream is almost boiling, stirring constantly. Remove from the heat and set to one side.

2 Whisk the egg yolks in a small mixing bowl. Whisk the warm cream into the egg yolks, a third at a time.

3 Pour the mixture back into the saucepan and return to a low heat. Stir until the custard has thickened. Do not allow it to boil. Once thickened, add the Splenda and allow to cool. Stir occasionally to prevent a skin forming.

4 Break the lemon sponge into a trifle bowl and stir in the raspberries.

5 Cover with the cooled custard and chill thoroughly.

6 Whip the remaining double cream until it is thickened and floppy, but not too stiff, and spread generously over the chilled trifle.

SERVES 4

CUSTARD
200ml double cream
100g good-quality dark (80% cocoa solids) chocolate, grated
4 egg yolks
2 tablespoons Splenda

SPONGE
2 large eggs, separated
60 ml double cream
1 tablespoon Splenda (optional)

A pinch of salt
2 heaped teaspoons good quality cocoa powder
120g ground almonds
1 teaspoon baking powder
2 tablespoons very strong decaf coffee

TO ASSEMBLE THE TRIFLE
250g raspberries, mashed with Splenda to taste
100g cherries, stoned and halved
60ml Kirsch
450ml double cream, whipped but slightly floppy
A sprinkling of grated chocolate

BLACK FOREST TRIFLE

1 To make the custard: place the double cream in a saucepan with the grated chocolate. Heat over a low to medium heat until the cream is almost boiling, stirring constantly. Remove from the heat and set to one side.

2 Whisk the egg yolks in a small mixing bowl. Whisk the warm cream into the egg yolks, a third at a time.

3 Pour the mixture back into the saucepan and return to a low heat. Stir until the custard has thickened. Do not allow the custard to boil. Once thickened add the Splenda and allow to cool. Stir occasionally to prevent a skin forming.

4 To make the sponge: put all the sponge ingredients into a large Pyrex bowl and stir until smooth. Cook on full power in a microwave for 3–4 minutes, or in the oven at 170°C/gas mark 3 for 20–30 minutes, until just springy to the touch. Allow to cool.

5 Cut the chocolate sponge into slices and sandwich together in pairs with the raspberry purée. Arrange in the bottom of a glass trifle dish, sprinkling over the cherry halves and Kirsch as you go.

6 Pour over the cooled chocolate custard, then cover the dish with clingfilm and chill for a couple of hours or overnight to allow it to thicken and set slightly.

7 Pile on the softly whipped double cream and decorate with grated chocolate.

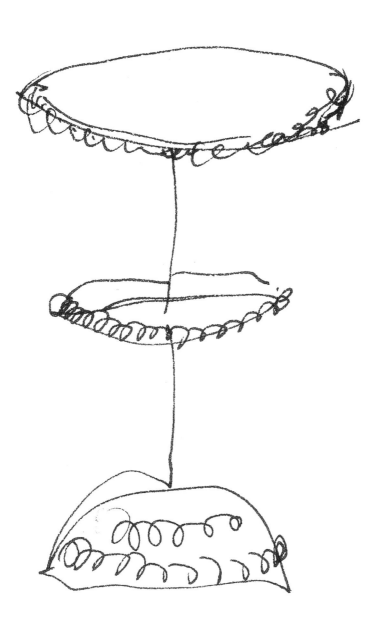

MAKES ABOUT 12
275g good-quality dark (70% plus
    cocoa solids) chocolate

250ml double cream
50g unsalted butter, cubed
2 tablespoons cocoa powder

CHOCOLATE TRUFFLES

1 Gently melt the chocolate in a bowl suspended over a pan of boiling water. Make sure the water doesn't touch the bottom of the bowl.

2 When the chocolate is melted, turn off the heat, stir in the double cream, and add the butter, little by little.

3 Put the whole thing into the fridge for a minimum of 4 hours, or overnight.

4 Remove the mixture from the fridge about 20 minutes before you're ready to start making the truffles. Sprinkle the cocoa powder on to a plate. With dry hands, shape the chocolate mixture into balls. Roll said balls in cocoa powder. Eat, or return them to the fridge until you want them. They keep about 2 days.

dark
chocolate
yum...

FOR EACH PERSON YOU NEED:
50g dark chocolate – at least 70% cocoa solids
1 egg, separated
1 teaspoon Splenda (optional)

CHOCOLATE MOUSSE

1 Sit a Pyrex bowl over a small saucepan of simmering water. Make sure the bottom of the bowl does not touch the water. Break the chocolate into small pieces, put them into the bowl and leave them to melt for about 5 minutes. Stir with a wooden spoon briefly to make sure everything has melted properly and the chocolate is smooth and glossy.

2 Add the egg yolk to the chocolate and beat in, still using the wooden spoon.

3 Using a spotlessly clean whisk and bowl, whip the egg white and Splenda (if using) until stiff peaks form. Fold the whipped egg white carefully but thoroughly into the chocolate mixture. Spoon into a ramekin or wineglass, cover and chill for about 2 hours until set.

4 Serve with double cream.

2 tablespoons soft fruit (strawberries, raspberries, blueberries, etc.)

2 scoops of vanilla ice cream (see page 216)

2 tablespoons sugar-free jelly

Softly whipped double cream

1 tablespoon toasted almonds

1 tablespoon grated dark chocolate

KNICKERBOCKER GLORY

You should really use a tall 'knickerbocker glory' glass for this, but any bowl will do.

1 All you do is alternate fruit, ice cream, jelly and cream, making sure that the top layer is cream, then sprinkle over the nuts and chocolate. Heaven.

MAKES 12

1 quantity basic almond sponge
    mixture (see page 215)
200g mascarpone cheese

Splenda to taste (optional)
1 teaspoon vanilla extract
Berries for decoration

CUPCAKES

1 Preheat the oven to 180°C/gas mark 4.

2 Make up the almond sponge mixture and use to fill 12 muffin
cases evenly. Bake in the oven for approximately 12 minutes,
or until golden brown and just firm to the touch.

3 Cool on a wire rack.

4 Beat together the mascarpone, Splenda (if using) and vanilla
extract until smooth and creamy. Divide this icing between the
cupcakes and level the tops.

5 Decorate with fresh berries.

CHAPTER FIFTEEN

BASICS

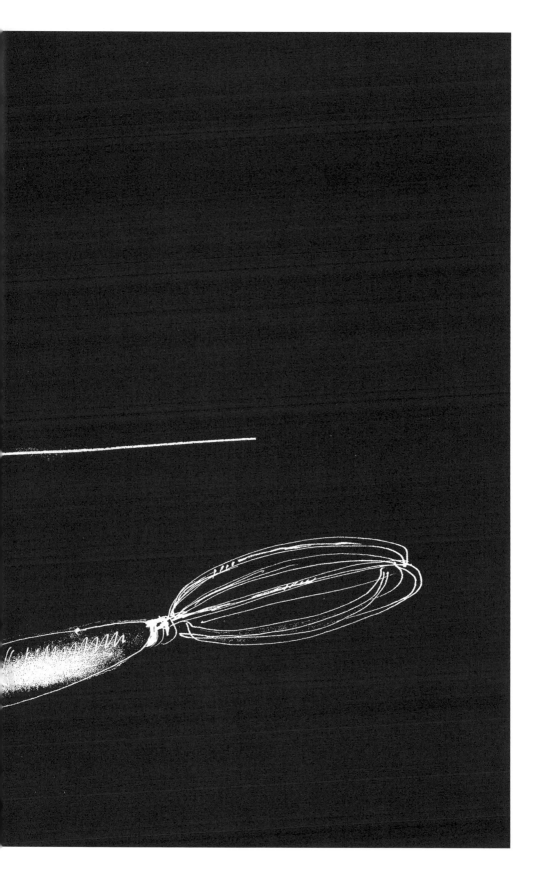

These are the staple recipes that you'll use again and again.

3 tablespoons oil
1 tablespoon vinegar
Salt and freshly ground black pepper

VINAIGRETTE

1 Whisk the oil and vinegar together until emulsified, then
season with salt and pepper. This is the basic formula for
vinaigrette. You can easily double or treble the quantities if you
want to make it in bulk – shake it vigorously in a screw-top jar
and store it in the fridge.

2 You can add other things for flavour and variety: lemon or lime
juice or zest, spices, chopped herbs, tomato purée, pesto, etc.

Salt + Pepper

1 cup of mayonnaise
1 cup of soured cream
Olive oil
Salt and freshly ground black pepper
A handful of crumbled blue cheese

BLUE CHEESE DRESSING

1 Blend the mayo with the cream. Add enough olive oil to make a dressing consistency, and season with salt and pepper. Stir in the blue cheese.

1 egg yolk
A pinch of mustard powder
A pinch of salt
140ml groundnut oil

MAYONNAISE

1 By far the easiest way to make this is to use a hand blender, a large jug to make it in and a small jug to pour the oil from.

2 Put the egg yolk into the large jug with the mustard powder and salt. Blitz with the hand blender.

3 With the blender running, carefully pour in a drip of oil from the small jug and move the hand blender up, down and around slightly to incorporate all the oil. Once half the oil has been added drip by drip you can add the rest in a steady stream, but continue to move the hand blender around. Once all the oil is in, if the mixture looks too thick you can whiz in a tablespoon of water, which will slacken the mayonnaise and also lighten the colour.

4 You can add many different things to mayonnaise: crushed garlic, horseradish, grainy mustard, pesto, tomato purée, blue cheese…

200g mascarpone cheese
50g grated Parmesan or other strong
    cheese
1/2 teaspoon mustard powder

CHEESE SAUCE

1 Place the mascarpone in a microwaveable dish and heat on full power for 1 minute.

2 Stir in the cheese and mustard powder and heat for another 30 seconds.

Oil or fat from a roast
1 medium onion, finely sliced
500ml vegetable or chicken stock

A 2cm slice of butternut squash, peeled
  and diced
Meat juices from a roast (optional)

BASIC GRAVY

1 Heat a tablespoon of oil or fat from a roast in a small saucepan
and fry the onion slowly until deep golden brown. Add the
stock, squash, meat juices and any sticky bits scraped from
the roasting tin, and bring to the boil. Simmer until the squash
is tender, then use a hand blender or food processor to blitz
until smooth.

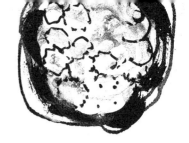

½ a cauliflower
A knob of butter
A glug of double cream
Salt and freshly ground black pepper
A little grated nutmeg, if you like

CAULIFLOWER FAUX-MASH

1 Steam the cauliflower florets until very tender. Chuck into a blender. Blend with a generous knob of butter and a glug of cream. Season with salt, pepper and nutmeg, and serve.

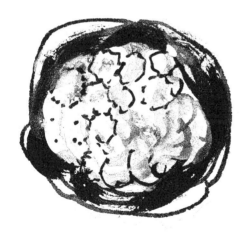

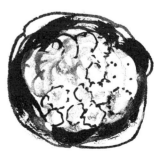

2 large eggs, separated
60ml double cream
2 tablespoons Splenda (optional)
50g melted butter

A pinch of salt
120ml ground almonds
1 teaspoon baking powder

BASIC ALMOND SPONGE

1 Preheat the oven to 180°C/gas mark 4.

2 In a large Pyrex bowl, mix together the egg yolks, cream, Splenda (if using), melted butter and salt until smooth. Whisk in the ground almonds and baking powder.

3 Place the egg whites in a separate bowl and beat with an electric mixer or hand whisk until soft peaks form. Stir a large spoonful of the whites into the almond mixture to loosen it up, then fold in the remaining whites.

4 Bake for 20–30 minutes (or cook on full power in a microwave for 4 minutes), until just springy to the touch.

500ml double cream
1 vanilla pod, split lengthways
5 large egg yolks
6 tablespoons Splenda

VANILLA ICE CREAM

1 Bring the cream and vanilla pod to the boil. Remove from the heat and set aside for 15 minutes to infuse. Whisk the egg yolks and Splenda together in a large bowl until pale and thick. Take out the vanilla pod and use a knife to scrape all the seeds back into the cream. Whisk the cream into the egg mixture.

2 Pour back into the pan and cook over a low heat for 4–5 minutes, until the custard coats the back of a wooden spoon – don't boil it or you will get sweet scrambled eggs. Strain into a bowl and cool.

3 Pour into an ice cream maker and churn until frozen, or pour into a plastic freezer box and freeze for about 4 hours, whisking really thoroughly every hour until half frozen and making sure there are no large ice crystals forming. Level the top and freeze until solid.

4 Before serving, remove from the freezer and put into the fridge for 30 minutes – this allows the ice cream to soften properly.

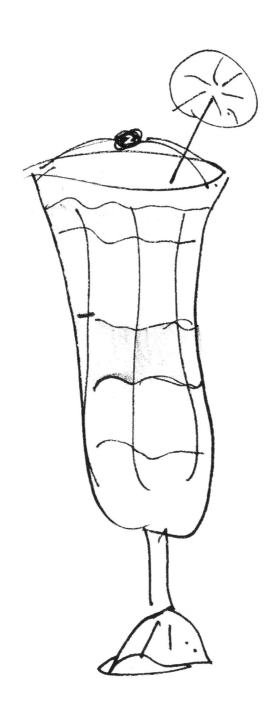

INDEX

Made with love from Bee, India and Nevis